# *The* LOST
# GOON SHOWS

£2·50

# The LOST GOON SHOWS

# SPIKE MILLIGAN

 Robson Books

*Goon Show admirers might like to know of:*

The Goon Show Preservation Society
24 Oakland Avenue
Hartlepool
Cleveland TS25 5LD
(Secretary: Christopher Smith)

Designed by Harold King

Drawings (mostly) by Spike Milligan

Thanks are owed to Mrs Larry Stephens for
permission to include 'Operation Christmas Duff'

This Robson paperback edition first published in 1993
First published in Great Britain in 1987 by Robson Books Ltd.,
Bolsover House, 5-6 Clipstone Street, London W1P 7EB.

**British Library Cataloguing in Publication Data**
A catalogue record for this title is available from the British
Library

ISBN 0 86051 460 9 (hbk)
        0 86051 887 6 (pbk)

Typeset by Bookworm Typesetting, Manchester. Printed in
Great Britain by St Edmundsbury Press Ltd., Bury St Edmunds,
Suffolk.

# CONTENTS

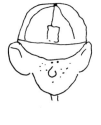

*Early days. The original quartet: Michael Bentine, Spike Milligan, Peter Sellers, Harry Secombe*

BBC

# INTRODUCTION

This, I presume, will be the last time some Goon Shows will go into print.

It's nigh on 35 years since that distant first show which, though full of enthusiasm, was pretty amateurish and really not very funny – however, we hung on in there and learned as we went along.

To my astonishment, I have discovered that there are Goon Show Preservation Societies all over Britain, Australia and America, and that the Goon Show is still being heard twice weekly in Australia, as it is in America. This makes it the longest-running comedy show ever, and I've written to the *Guinness Book of Records* informing them. They ignore my letters, so I've stopped drinking Guinness.

After all these years, these 'lost' Goon Shows didn't seem that funny to me and I've rewritten here and there to jolly them up a little. I hope they jolly you up a little.

p.s. Since writing this, I have discovered an unfinished Goon Show
  – for some reason never completed and therefore never performed. Alas, with Sellers gone, it never can be. But though it's too late, it's not too late to include it in this little volume.

*Spike Milligan*

SPIKE MILLIGAN

BBC

Spike Milligan with Larry Stephens, his collaborator on
'Operation Christmas Duff'

# OPERATION CHRISTMAS DUFF

The Goon Show: Special Overseas Edition
Recorded 9th December 1956
First Transmission 24th December, 1956 (General Overseas Service only)
Second Transmission Christmas Day, 1986 (Radio 4)

# Cast (main characters)

**Spike Milligan**
>    Statisticker
>    Sparks
>    Seaman
>    Batman
>    Captain Berk
>    Eccles
>    Moriarty

**Peter Sellers**
>    Minister of Military-type Foods
>    Dimbleby .
>    Major Bloodnok
>    Churchill
>    Bluebottle
>    Grytpype

**Harry Secombe**
>    Admiral Seagoon
>    Captain Thing

With The Ray Ellington Quartet, Max Geldray, and the
Orchestra conducted by Wally Stott.
Script by Spike Milligan and Larry Stephens.
Announcer Wallace Greenslade.
Producer Pat Dixon.

Entrusted with the task of driving a giant Christmas pudding to the Forces Overseas (minus one slice destined for the Trans-Antarctic Expedition), Eccles and Bluebottle run into trouble in the shape of two starving ne'er-do-wells, Moriarty and Grytpype. Meanwhile, in the icy arctic wastes, their strength ebbing away, Admiral Seagoon and Major Bloodnok are on the horns of a classic dilemma: whether to have their pudding, or eat it. The choice is agonizing . . .

**WALLACE**    This programme is specially dedicated to Her Majesty's Forces Overseas and to the Trans-Antarctic Expedition, the Falkland Islands Dependency Survey Teams, the Royal Society Expedition at Halle Bay, and Mrs Rita Body. Greetings from the Goons.

**ECCLES**    Hallo.

**ORCHESTRA**    *Regal fanfare*

**PETER**    This is the story of a great endeavour.

**ECCLES**    Is it?

**PETER**    A story of land, sea and air. And in some cases, both. The date: the 23rd November 1956. Christmas was coming. The geese were getting fat. Someone spent a penny in an old man's hat. But one problem lay heavily on Parliament's conscience.

| | |
|---|---|
| **FX** | *(fade in) Crowd of Greeks talking* |
| **MINISTER** | Gentlemen – as Minister of Military-type Foods, I must say the picture regarding Christmas puddings for the forces overseas looks pretty black. |
| **MP** | Why don't we send them black puddings? |
| **ORCHESTRA** | *Corny chord* |
| **PETER** | Thank you, Sir Hartley Shawcross KC. And now, a few statistics from our resident statisticker. |
| **ORCHESTRA** | *Lively introductory-type music* |
| **STATISTICKER** | I say, I say, I say. I say, gentlemen, owing to the shortage of civilian compressors, they cannot supply sufficient Xmas-type duff for our forces overseas. |
| **OLD MAN** | What about the Naafi? |
| **FIRST VOICE** | Naafi – what is Naafi? |
| **SECOND VOICE** | An organization working for the downfall of the British Army. |
| **STATISTICKER** | Gentlemen, gentlemen, I have a solution. I just took it off a bicycle tyre. Now, listen to me, please. Why don't the services all combine in the building of a giant Services Christmas pudding? |
| **FX** | *Crowd – applause, cheers, fade in singing of 'Land of Hope and Glory'* |
| **PETER** | The motion was adopted and passed. But meanwhile, at the Admiralty – |
| **FX** | *Bosun's whistle* |

**SPARKS**  Pardon me, sir RN.

**SEAGOON**  What is it?

**SPARKS**  I am sorry to interrupt you at squash, sir.

**SEAGOON**  It's all right, I'll drink it later.

**SPARKS**  This morse signal's just arrived from Magadan Trans-Antarctic Expedition, sir.

**SEAGOON**  What does it say?

**SPARKS**  I don't know, it's all little dots and dashes.

**SEAGOON**  Play it on the gramophone.

**SPARKS**  Right. (*Beeping sound*) Is it code?

Neddie
Seagon

SEAGOON   Yes – stoke up the fire. (*Morse code bleeping continues*) Of course! It's in Morse – I speak it fluently. It's We-Want-a-Christmas-Pudding-for-Christmas-by-the-boys-of-the-Trans-Antarctic-Expedition with-Taffy-Williams-at-the-Mighty-Morse-Keys. Gad, it means those lads out there in all that sand and snow are pudding-less!

SPARKS   I fear so, sir.

SEAGOON   It's not British, I tell you, it's not British.

SPARKS   No, sir – most Christmas puddings are made-in-Japan pluddings.

SEAGOON   Wait! I have it!

SPARKS   Yes, I can see you've got it, sir.

SEAGOON   We will have to ask the service chiefs to increase the size of the giant Service Christmas pudding to allow for an extra slice for the Antarctic base.

SPARKS   Yes, sir. E'en now they're mixing it at Chatham. I'll drive you there.

FX   *Whip cracks. Two men running away*

GRAMS   *'Claire de Lune'*

WALLACE   We included that brief excerpt from 'Claire de Lune' for people who speak French. Now, over to Richard Dimbleby.

FX   *Machinery – very complicated, spurts, plops etc*

● ● ● ● ● ● ● ● ● ● ● ● ●

| | |
|---|---|
| **DIMBLEBY** | The sound you are now hearing is the combined Services Christmas pudding in the making. I am standing by the great dry dock at Chatham in which the Christmas pudding is being mixed. Standing next to me, two feet lower down is Admiral Seagoon. |
| *FX* | *Bosun's whistle* |
| **SEAGOON** | Ah, that's better! Well, we've had a good day for pudding. Number three flotilla torpedo boats have been going backwards and forwards churning up the mixture. The cruiser Ajax has been following in their wake, dropping depth charges to bring the raisins to the surface. |
| **DIMBLEBY** | The finest traditions of the silent service being maintained. |
| *FX* | *Bosun's whistle* |
| **SEAGOON** | Ah, that's better! Yes, yes, we try to keep the men happy when they're off duty by giving them little tasks like this. |
| **DIMBLEBY** | We could do with more of that spirit. |
| **SEAMAN** | (*uncouth*) You could both do with a big clout up the back of your big fat steaming nuts. |
| **SEAGOON** | Our nuts are not steaming – arrest that stoker. |
| **DIMBLEBY** | How do you test the density of this great Service pudding? |
| **SEAGOON** | We sent a diver down half an hour ago. It was silly, really. |

● ● ● ● ● ● ● ● ● ● ● ● ● ● 15

BBC

| | |
|---|---|
| **DIMBLEBY** | Why? |
| **SEAGOON** | He hasn't got a diving suit on, ha ha – he he! |
| **DIMBLEBY** | (*very earnest*) The best tradition of the Navy cake! |
| *FX* | *Aeroplane* |
| **DIMBLEBY** | And now the great dockyard is being cleared, as the fairy gannets of 824 Squadron swoop low over the pudding. Their bomb bays are open, and yes, down comes the candied peel, ginger and sultanas. |

| | |
|---|---|
| *FX* | *Bomb descending, and crash* |
| **DIMBLEBY** | A direct hit on the great Christmas pudding mixture! A grand day for the Royal Air Force and Miss Muriel Body. |
| **SEAMAN** | Pardon me, sir, oil tankers standing by to take on the pudding! |
| **SEAGOON** | Right – drop the suction pumps into the mixture and suck it! |
| **SEAMAN** | (*off*) Aye aye, sir. |
| *FX* | *Suction pump, slurping noises* |
| **DIMBLEBY** | And so the great pudding mixture is siphoned out of the dry dock and into the all-British oil tanker, *Aristotle Onassis,* which is registered as a bakery in Rangoon. |
| **SEAGOON** | Yes, it'll be transported overland to an empty gasometer near Salisbury Plain. From then the pudding is under Army command. Unfortunately. |
| **DIMBLEBY** | Thank you, Admiral Seagoon. Now over to Max Geldray for some rum and baccy. |
| ***MAX AND ORCHESTRA*** | *Music* |
| **WALLACE** | Operation Christmas Duff, Part Two. |

| | |
|---|---|
| *FX* | *Bugle call all wrong* |
| **BLOODNOK** | Oh, it's – er – what is it? Of course, it's reveille. And first thing in the morning, too. What a shock. Quick, batman – brandy – brandy! |
| **BATMAN** | Have you got a weak heart? |
| **BLOODNOK** | No, a weak will. |
| **BATMAN** | Oh! So have I, sir. (*Drinking*) |
| **BLOODNOK** | Put that bottle down! |
| **BATMAN** | I'm trying to, sir. |
| **BLOODNOK** | Give me that. (*Drinking*) |
| *FX* | *Tap dripping* |
| **BATMAN** | You're leaking, sir. |
| **CAPTAIN THING** | Major! 0600 hours, sir, transporter arrived with converted gasometer with 600 tons of Christmas pudding ready for cooking, sir! |
| **BLOODNOK** | Oh, Captain Thing! What's its map reference? |
| **CAPTAIN THING** | 7981 – Salisbury Plain, sir! |
| **BLOODNOK** | Where's that? |
| **CAPTAIN THING** | You're standing on it, sir! |
| **BLOODNOK** | I'm sorry, I hope I haven't dirtied it. |

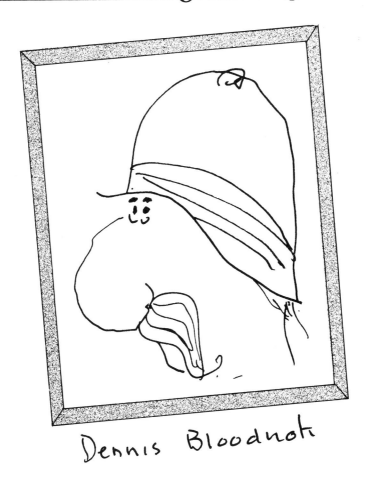

Dennis Bloodnok

**CAPTAIN THING**  It's all right, sir! We have it blanco'd every other day.

**FX**  *Knocks at door*

**CAPTAIN THING**  Knocks on door, sir!

**BLOODNOK**  Come in! – Two! – Three!

**FX**  *Navy whistle*

**SEAGOON**   Ah, that's better!

**BLOODNOK**   Oh, it's an Admiral. What are you doing so far on military land?

**SEAGOON**   I ran aground, sir. I was sent along to report on the cooking.

**BLOODNOK**   Follow me. (*Footsteps*) The Derbyshire Yeomanry have laid on fourteen flame-throwing tanks.

**FX**   Bugle – 'Come to the cook-house door'. *Mad stampede of soldiers*

**SEAGOON**   I say, what call is that?

**BLOODNOK**   Cook-house! Number one on our hit parade, you know. Has been for three hundred years. If you'll just come into this observation post you'll be able to watch the whole of the Christmas pudding being cooked. Let's go over to the radar screen.

**FX**   Electronic noises. Flame-throwers. Tanks

**WALLACE**   Hello, listeners. The sound you're hearing are the tanks which are bringing their flame-throwers to bear, as they cook the giant Christmas pudding in its gasometer.

**CAPTAIN BERK**   At dawn this morning, number forty-five commando went in under cover of daylight, and brought back samples for testing by the Army Catering Corps.

**WALLACE**   What was it like?

**CAPTAIN BERK**   Pretty good.

| | |
|---|---|
| **BLOODNOK** | Ah, Captain Berk. |
| **CAPTAIN BERK** | Two, three, four, Sah! |
| **BLOODNOK** | Field Intelligence reports that the pudding is done. |
| **CAPTAIN BERK** | Absolutely first class. I should wait till things have cooled down a bit, then send in the Sappers to blast open the gasometer with Bangalore torpedoes. |
| **WALLACE** | Excuse me, Major, I'm from the BBC. |
| **BLOODNOK** | I'm sorry, I don't have any money on me. |
| *FX* | *Distant atom bomb* |
| **BLOODNOK** | Oh, there she goes! You see that? Split the gasometer completely in two. Well done, Sappers. |
| **WALLACE** | Indeed, listeners. Right in two, revealing a great, steaming, Services Christmas pudding. |
| *FX* | *Gunfire* |
| **WALLACE** | And there you hear the 74th Medium Regiment RA firing over open sights smack into the pudding itself. Tell me, Major, what are they firing? |
| **BLOODNOK** | Threepenny bits. |
| **CAPTAIN BERK** | Excuse me, sir, the infantry CO is on the walkie-talkie. |
| **BLOODNOK** | Hello? Sunray here. |

**SEAGULL**   Seagull speaking – sit. rep., sir. B Company 2nd Force have reached the summit of the Christmas pudding.

**BLOODNOK**   Right, consolidate! Roger and out. Gentlemen, the Army's task in this matter is completed. It is now under RAF command. Unfortunately.

*GRAMS*   'Dam Busters March'

**HARRY**   That night, an excited House was given the news.

*FX*   Crowd noise – heavy mutterings – occasional chicken

**CHURCHILL**   Honourable members, I have this moment received good news. At 1700 hours British troops gained the summit of the combined Services Christmas pudding and there planted the British holly.

*FX*   Applause and cheers

**CHURCHILL**   One hour later, the Canberras of Bomber Command dropped delayed custard bombs, followed by brandy torpedoes – then napalm to set it alight.

*FX*   Cheers – all sing 'Land of Hope and Glory'

**WALLACE**   Late that night, Service chiefs were given their instructions at the War Office.

*FX*   Bar room noises – honky tonk piano, drunken singing, 'Oh Danny Boy' etc

**SEAGOON**   Gentlemen, please, please. If the Chief of the Imperial General Staff will lay off the piano! Thank you. I have here sealed orders containing four tickets for the

Windmill, and this message: 'The pudding will be divided as follows: One slice to be cut and filled with anti-freeze for immediate transport to the Trans-Antarctic expedition. The remainder of the giant Christmas pudding will be fitted with wheels, a diesel engine, and driven to the Middle East depots for distribution. Signed, Field Marshal Montgoonery.'

**GRAMS** *Eastern music*

**FX** *Sand storm. Heavy vehicle struggling over terrain*

**BLUEBOTTLE** Have you ever driven a Christmas pudding before?

**ECCLES** No, I never driven **anything** before.

**BLUEBOTTLE** Then how did you get the job?

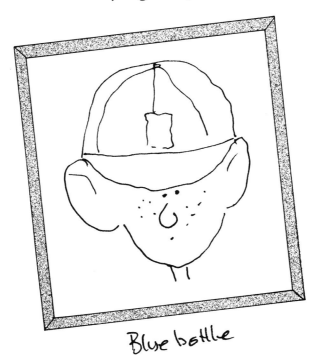

Blue bottle

Eccles

ECCLES          The Sergeant said, one pace forward anyone who can play the piano.

BLUEBOTTLE      Oh. Can you play the piano then?

ECCLES          No.

BLUEBOTTLE      Then why are you driving this Christmas pudding?

ECCLES          I want to learn to play the piano.

BLUEBOTTLE      Then it's **true** what the recruiting posters say.

ECCLES          What do they say?

BLUEBOTTLE      'You're **somebody** in the modern army of today'.

ECCLES          Oh. And what are you?

BLUEBOTTLE      I'm somebody in the modern army of today.

**ECCLES**      Oh. I wondered who you were. How did you join?

**BLUEBOTTLE**  I was in the street writing something on the wall. I was only writing my name.

**ECCLES**      Wouldn't they know who done it then?

**BLUEBOTTLE**  No, I didn't sign it. Then up comes a naughty hairy man wearing a soldier set, and he said 'Little Finchley lad, you don't want to write your name in little silly chalk. You want to write your name in ink.' And then I said 'Where?' And he said 'On this nice military dotted line.' So I signed it. Then they said 'Can you play the piano?' and I said 'Yes.' And here I am.

**ECCLES**      Give us a tune.

**BLUEBOTTLE**  What would you like?

**ECCLES**      My ticket.

**BLUEBOTTLE**  How does it go?

**ECCLES**      It goes (*sings*): Doctor, my dear military doctor, you gotta believe me, I got a bad back in the front. I'm not fit for active service, I gotta bone in my leg. And when I close my eyes I can't see. When I lie down it hurts me to lie sideways (*he fades away enumerating diseases*).

**QUARTET**     *'Old Man River'*

**GRYTPYPE**    Moriarty —

**MORIARTY**   (*toothless*) What? Can't you see I'm busy licking a jam spoon?

**GRYTPYPE**   Tell us who we are.

Grytpype-Thynne

**MORIARTY**   This **us** is Moriarty, and this us is Grytpype.

**GRYTPYPE**   What's that coming round the mountain pass in Cyrenaica?

**MORIARTY**   Hand me my telescopic wig, I'll just trim the fringe.

**FX**   *Scissors*

**MORIARTY**   Ah yes. Sapristi pompet! It's a giant Christmas puddding with a sign on top that says 'Low Bridge'.

**GRYTPYPE**   Anything else?

**MORIARTY**   Yes, a low bridge. This is our big chance!

● ● ● ● ● ● ● ● ● ● ● ●

**GRYTPYPE**   Big chance – to what?

**MORIARTY**   Ooh, to **eat!!!** Give me my teeth back!

**GRYTPYPE**   You can't have them, Moriarty, they're mine forever. You should never have left France for the National Health colonic irrigation!

**MORIARTY**   We must get to that pudding before Christmas or it will be out of date.

Moriarty

**GRYTPYPE**   Right, first we must stop them, Moriarty. Now, you stand in the road and raise your kilt. No! Not that much! It may be a lady driver.

**FX**   *Screeching tyres*

**GRYTPYPE**   Dear Moriarty, she pulled up –

**MORIARTY**   I know (*laughs*).

**GRYTPYPE**   (*laughing*) And I ruined the gag . . .

**HARRY**    And I'll continue as if nothing has happened.

**BLUEBOTTLE**    Oh, little thin man, are you ill?

**MORIARTY**    Yes! Only one thing can save poor old Moriarty's life.

**GRYTPYPE**    Yes, let me speak – I'm his guru – he **must** have a diet of **military** Christmas pudding, which he must eat on the move.

**ECCLES**    Oh, yer! Christmas pudding will keep you on the move all right.

**BLUEBOTTLE**    And we're driving one on the move.

**GRYTPYPE**    Good, help me get him and his starvation inside.

**OMNES**    *(grunting, etc)*

**WALLACE**    Elsewhere, the portion of the pudding destined for the Antarctic base was on board the SS Phyllis, going full steam ahead through the ice floes.

**FX**    *Wind and sea. Breaking of ice*

**BLOODNOK**    Gad, what a night on board – nothing but sleep. I tell you it's freezing out there. Mine are all shrivelled up!

**SEAGOON**    Keep your chin up, Major.

**BLOODNOK**    Why?

**SEAGOON**    It's in the soup.

**BLOODNOK**    I'm sorry, I thought my beard was on fire.

| | |
|---|---|
| **SEAMAN** | Land ahead! |
| **SEAGOON** | They've sighted the ice shelf. Gad, in a few days we'll be at the base with the pudding. What a thrill it will be. I can see Dr Foulkes' face now. |
| **BLOODNOK** | You've got damned good eyesight. |
| **SEAGOON** | Prepare to unload pudding, dogs and sleds. |
| *ORCHESTRA* | *Dramatic chords* |
| *FX* | *Yapping dogs – grunting* |
| **SEAGOON** | It was hellish work pulling our pudding on the ice. |
| **WALLACE** | Seven months later as the crow flies, a line of dialogue. |
| **BLOODNOK** | Oh Seagoon, I'm knackered! What's the time? |
| **SEAGOON** | I can't tell until it gets dark. |
| **BLOODNOK** | Why? |
| **SEAGOON** | My watch has got a luminous dial. |
| **BLOODNOK** | Curse. We shall have to wait till nightfall before we know it's dark. |
| **SEAGOON** | Good God! We've run out of food! |
| **BLOODNOK** | We've still got the Christmas pudding. |
| **SEAGOON** | Stop! You touch that, Bloodnok, and I'll – That's for the boys at the Antarctic base. |

| | |
|---|---|
| **BLOODNOK** | But if we don't eat it we won't have the strength to pull it. |
| **SEAGOON** | I knew he was right. All right! Just a thin quarter-ounce slice each. |
| **BLOODNOK** | Can't I have a **thick** quarter-ounce slice? |
| **SEAGOON** | No, but I'll meet you halfway. |
| **BLOODNOK** | All right, I'll see you there then. |
| **ORCHESTRA** | *Dramatic chords* |
| **FX** | *Icy wind — howling gale — distant howling wolves* |
| **WALLACE** | Log of expedition. |

| | |
|---|---|
| FX | *Sound of nib scratching paper* |
| SEAGOON | December 52nd. Took off record of effects. (*FX cease*) For three nights now gallant Bloodnok has volunteered to stay awake and guard the pudding. |
| FX | *Sound of nib scratching paper* |
| BLOODNOK | December 1st. Pudding getting smaller. |
| FX | *Sound of nib scratching paper* |
| SEAGOON | Bloodnok getting bigger. |
| FX | *Scratchy nib as before* |
| BLOODNOK | Seagoon getting suspicious. |
| FX | *Scratchy nib* |
| SEAGOON | December 19th! |
| FX | *Writing as before* |
| BLOODNOK | Oo-ooh! |
| FX | *Writing* |
| SEAGOON | Caught Bloodnok red-handed digging into the pudding. |
| BLOODNOK | It's a lie! I'm brown handed! |
| SEAGOON | Bloodnok – you fool, you devil. Open your hand. |
| FX | *Coins hit floor* |
| SEAGOON | Ah, so that's what you're after. Threepenny bits! |

**BLOODNOK**   Yes, I wanted to make a phone call.

**SEAGOON**   Phones? Here? Ha ha!

*FX*   *Phone rings*

**SEAGOON**   *(insane)* Don't answer it! It's – it's a mirage.

**BLOODNOK**   Mirages don't ring – it's a phone.

**SEAGOON**   You can't out-act me! It's – a – **PHONE!**

**BLOODNOK**   Nonsense. *(Picks up phone)* Hello??

**DISTORTED VOICE**   Hello, this is a mirage speaking.

*FX*   *Phone crashed down*

**BLOODNOK**   Oo-oh! You were right, Seagoon. Oh, unless we reach the base soon my mind will die of starvation!

*FX*   *Duck quacks*

**BLOODNOK**   It's the phone again – ohh!

**SEAGOON**   Rubbish, ducks don't ring.

*FX*   *Lorry drives up and stops*

**ECCLES**   Hello, boys. We've brought you your Christmas pudding.

**BLOODNOK**   It's a mirage!

**SEAGOON**   What, what, what, what, what?

**ECCLES**   Hello dere – phew, what a scorcher!

● ● ● ● ● ● ● ● ● ● ● ● ●

**SEAGOON** The voice came from an idiot in a vest and sun helmet pouring with sweat.

**ECCLES** Here, I bet this is the first time you've had snow in Libya.

**BLOODNOK** **Libya??** It's a mirage –

**SEAGOON** Nonsense! According to my calculations and our position on the map, we are twenty miles south of here.

**BLOODNOK** Well, we shall soon settle this. Let's ask this mirage. Excuse me, sir, where's our position?

**FRENCHMAN** Cher monsieur, soyez le bienvenu à New York.

**BLOODNOK** He says, 'Welcome to New York'

**SEAGOON** Nonsense. Mirages don't speak French.

**ECCLES** What's New York doing in Libya?

**BLOODNOK** You mean, what's New York doing in the Antarctic?

**ECCLES** Wot's der Antarctic doing in Libya?

**BLOODNOK** Perhaps it's on holiday.

**ECCLES** This time of the year?

**SEAGOON** Will you stop talking rubbish?

**ECCLES** Have you got a piano?

**BLOODNOK** Well, we'll soon settle where we are. I'll just toss this coin (*sound of coin spinning*). Ah. Heads! We are in Mongolia!

**SEAGOON**  Ah. But you're using a Mongolian penny.

**BLOODNOK**  Only one side.

**SEAGOON**  What does that mean?

**BLOODNOK**  It means, we're on one side of Mongolia.

**ECCLES**  I want to learn the piano.

**SEAGOON**  What are you talking about?

**ECCLES**  About ten words a minute

**ALL THREE**  (*Arguing*)

**SEAGOON**  Stop! Stop! – I know – it's **me** – **I'm** a mirage – that's it! **Help – help!!!**

**WALLACE**  (*talks over Seagoon's babbling*) Ladies and gentlemen, you've been listening to a series of mirages called the Goon Show – it will be cold tonight with a frost.

**ECCLES**  Here, I found a piano –

**FX**  *Terrible piano fade out into Arctic winds – in the distance we hear Bloodnok and Seagoon accusing each other of being a mirage.*

BBC

*In control as ever – producer Dennis Main Wilson*

BBC

# THE INTERNAL MOUNTAIN

▶ ▶ ▶ 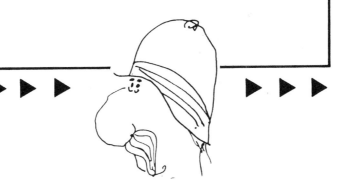 ▶ ▶ ▶

The Goon Show: 'Vintage Goons', No. 9
Recorded 16th February, 1958
First Transmission 28th December, 1986 (Radio 4)

# Cast (main characters)

**Spike Milligan**
> The Spirit of Adventure
> Eccles
> Minnie Bannister
> Moriarty
> Jim Spriggs

**Peter Sellers**
> Cronk
> Henry Crun
> Grytpype
> Major Bloodnok
> Bluebottle

**Harry Secombe**
> Lord Hairy Seagoon

With The Ray Ellington Quartet, Max Geldray, and the Orchestra
conducted by Wally Stott.
Announcer Wallace Greenslade.
Producer Charles Chilton.

▶ ▶ ▶ ▶ ▶ ▶ ▶ ▶ ▶ ▶ ▶ ▶ ▶ ▶

Ever in search of fresh adventures and new horizons, restless man of action Lord Hairy Seagoon sets himself the ultimate challenge: to climb Mount Everest *from the inside*. With a little ingenious help from Major Bloodnok, Seagoon succeeds in planting a Union Jack on the summit, only to find that there is truth in the old saying, 'It is better to travel hopefully than to arrive'.

**WALLACE**  This is the BBC, natural inheritor of the alphabet ABC. Tonight's programme comes to you by arrangement with the makers of Kiddies Head Crushing Machines Ltd. We present Sita Fellers, Natty Floorcloth and Mike Middington in The Goon Show.

**ORCHESTRA**  *Dramatic chords*

**WALLACE**  This is a story of high adventure, one that will blaze its way across the lingth, length and longth of Great Britain, Ireland, Scotland, Wales, England and Scunthorpe.

**HARRY**  This story will swell with pride the feet of every true Englishman, woman, child, cat, dog, chicken, to say nothing of Footo, the Wonder Boot Exploder!

**FX**  *Explosion. Scream*

**SPIKE**  Listeners may well ask what Footo the Wonder Boot Exploder has to do with our story. Well, **we shall see, ha ha!**

**WALLACE**  Now to the drama. The –

**HARRY**  Let me – the saga of The Internal Mountain.

| | |
|---|---|
| *FX* | *Chickens. Bagpipes. Splash. Chickens* |
| | *Pause)* |
| **SPIKE** | **We shall see.** |
| *ORCHESTRA* | *Dramatic chords* |
| **SEAGOON** | The Internal Mountain. Ha ha! How well I remember it. But first things first. My name is Lord Hairy Seagoon, Doctor of Philosophy and spinster of this parish. I am six foot three except on television. A man of action. Yes, I've rubbed shoulders with death. I've knocked on doors and run away. Oh, you may not believe this, I've run through Piccadilly without my underpants. |
| **VOICE** | *(gay)* You devil! |
| **WALLACE** | One night, as Lord Hairy lay tossing and turning in his egg box, under the stairs of Ronnie Scott's Jazz Club Anonymous – a mystic ethereal voice spoke to him. |
| *GRAMS* | *Harp – glissando* |
| **GHOSTLY VOICE** | Lord Seagoon, Seagoon. Can you hear me? Over. |
| **SEAGOON** | Yes, yes. I hear you strength three. Roger. |
| **GHOSTLY VOICE** | This is not Roger. It is Fred Toley, the spirit of adventure. Now living abroad owing to tax. |
| **SEAGOON** | *(laughing)* You sound like Milligan through a megaphone. |
| **GHOSTLY VOICE** | Listen, I come to gratify your desire. If you seek new horizons, climb Mount Everest. |

▶ ▶ ▶ ▶ ▶ ▶ ▶ ▶ ▶ ▶ ▶ ▶ ▶ ▶

**SEAGOON**   Oh spirit there, it has already been clumbed.

**GHOSTLY VOICE**   It has not been clumbed from the **inside!**

**SEAGOON**   The **inside?** Oh spirit, you are right!

**GHOSTLY VOICE**   I must go now. I see my last tram coming.

**SEAGOON**   Wait, wait! Curses, the spirit has gone. It must have been only 70% proof. Climb Everest from the **inside?** It's never been done before. Cronk!

BBC

CRONK     Yes, my lord?

SEAGOON     Lay out my purple serge suit, yellow and black polka dot tie, green and mauve striped shirt, gold monogrammed boots, white bowler, and pink hand-painted souzaphone.

CRONK     Another funeral, sir?

SEAGOON     No, not today. I'm going to the Royal Alpine Club.

CRONK     I'll phone your office and tell them you won't be in.

SEAGOON     Yes, they'll have to try and manage without me.

FX     *Dialling phone number*

CRONK     Hello? Sir Bernard? Lord Seagoon's compliments, sir, he will not be in today.

FX     *Replaces phone*

SEAGOON     Well?

CRONK     You are fired, sir.

SEAGOON     Ha! Ha! I shouldn't worry about a job with my qualifications. Let them get another lift attendant.

CRONK     Spoken like a true failure.

SEAGOON     Mark my words, Cronk, he'll never get another man like me.

CRONK     That's what he said, sir. I never want another man like you.

SEAGOON     Is my horseless carriage ready?

▶ ▶ ▶ ▶ ▶ ▶ ▶ ▶ ▶ ▶ ▶ ▶ ▶ ▶ ▶

**CRONK**   The chauffeur is pulling it here now.

*FX*   *Car horn*

**ECCLES**   Hello. The car's ready.

**SEAGOON**   Good lad, Eccles. Here's a sugar lump. That's what I like – car right outside my door.

**ECCLES**   Yer, but you never told me you lived on the twentieth floor.

**SEAGOON**   All right, Eccles – the Alpine Club.

*FX*   *Footsteps running away*

**SEAGOON**   I'd better follow him in the car.

*FX*   *Boots running away*

**ORCHESTRA**   *'The Lambeth Walk'*

**WALLACE**   With that inexplicable music, Seagoon arrives at the Royal Alpine Club.

*FX*   *Knocking on door*

**CRUN**   Kanchenjunga, 22,000 feet ...

*FX*   *Hammering on door*

**MINNIE**   Henry?

*FX*   *More hammering*

**CRUN**   What, Min?

**MINNIE**   There's someone knocking at the door.

Henry Crun

**CRUN**   Which side, Min?

Minnie Bannister

**MINNIE**   Outside.

*FX*   *Knocking*

**MINNIE**   There it is again, Henry.

**CRUN**   He must be trying to get in.

**SEAGOON**   (*shouting*) Hello in there! I'm sorry, I happened to be knocking – I thought I'd call in.

**CRUN**   What is it, Min?

**MINNIE**   There was someone knocking at the door who thought he'd call in.

*FX*   *Door opens*

**SEAGOON**   Save your breath.

**MINNIE**   I have been saving it for years, it mounts up, you know.

**CRUN**   Please come in, whoever knocks.

**SEAGOON**   But I tell you –

▶ ▶ ▶ ▶ ▶ ▶ ▶ ▶ ▶ ▶ ▶ ▶ ▶ ▶ ▶

CRUN       Please don't interrupt the private affairs of the house. Is there someone knocking at the door?

SEAGOON    *(shouting)* Yes!

CRUN       *(shouting)* Who?

SEAGOON    *(yells)* Me!

CRUN       *(yells)* Then **come** in.

SEAGOON    *(shouts)* I **am** in.

CRUN       *(angry)* Then what are you knocking for?

SEAGOON    *(furious)* I'm not knocking!
CRUN       Then how do you expect us to know you're there? Who are you, little dwarf?

SEAGOON    I'm Lord Seagoon.

CRUN       It's Lord Seagoon, Min. What can we do for you, little dwarf?

SEAGOON    I want the Alphine Club to cooperate in climbing Mount Everest from the inside.

CRUN       Who would finance such a thing?

SEAGOON    **Me**! Would you mind turning your back while I unfasten my money belt?

FX         *Padlock and chains. Hacksaw. Bolts being withdrawn. Creaking hinges*

SEAGOON    Oh – it was open all the time.

| | |
|---|---|
| **MINNIE** | Can we turn round now? |
| **SEAGOON** | Yes. There is the money. Feast your eyes. |
| **CRUN** | Two shillings? |
| **SEAGOON** | Isn't that enough? I have another threepence in my boot, which I can explode with Footo the Wonder Boot Exploder. |
| **CRUN** | It's not enough. You'll need at least in the neighbourhood of a pound. |
| **SEAGOON** | A pound. It sounds like a rich neighbourhood. |
| **CRUN** | It is. I know a money lender there. |
| **SEAGOON** | A money lender? I suppose he works under a nom de plume? |
| **CRUN** | Yes, and in the summer the pong is terrible! |
| **SEAGOON** | I'll go and see him. Max Geldray – play me there on your nose support. |
| **MAX** | Ploogie |
| **MAX AND ORCHESTRA** | *Music* |
| **WALLACE** | The Internal Mountain Climbers, page 3, 4, 5, 6 and etc. Enter Seagoon in cloak, paper hat and hedgehog-skin jock strap. He approaches door of money lender and knocks. |
| **FX** | *Doorbell* |

Max Geldray

*A heavily disguised Max Geldray, circa 1980*

| SEAGOON | Blast! |
|---|---|
| **GRYTPYPE** | Come in, Seagoon, |
| *FX* | *Door opens and closes* |
| **SEAGOON** | Good morning, nom de plume. I wish to borrow X pounds. |
| **GRYTPYPE** | X pounds? What for? |
| **SEAGOON** | X penses! Ha ha ha! Just my little joke. |
| *FX* | *Gunshot* |
| **GRYTPYPE** | Just my little bullet. Now, dear ragged Ned, sit on this blank cheque and tell me all. |
| **SEAGOON** | I want to borrow thirty thousand pounds. |
| *FX* | *Cascade of coins* |
| **SEAGOON** | All in farthings? |
| **GRYTPYPE** | Moriarty – |
| **MORIARTY** | What do you want, Grytpype, what do you want? Can't you see I'm busy painting the *Queen Elizabeth?* |
| **GRYTPYPE** | Parcel up the gentleman's money. Neddy, just sign this gentleman's agreement, please. |
| **SEAGOON** | Let me see it. (*Unfolds paper*) I promise to pay back thirty thousand pounds, plus **ten thousand?** |

▶ ▶ ▶ ▶ ▶ ▶ ▶ ▶ ▶ ▶ ▶ ▶ ▶ ▶ ▶ ▶

| | |
|---|---|
| **GRYTPYPE** | That's the tip, Neddy. |
| **SEAGOON** | I refuse to sign. |
| *GRAMS* | *Harp – ghostly glissando* |
| **GHOSTLY VOICE** | Seagoon – I am the tooth fairy spirit come to help. Sign it with a false name. |
| **SEAGOON** | Of course. Very well. (*Signs paper*) There. Miss Rita Body – that'll fool 'em. |
| **GRYTPYPE** | So you're a woman? |
| **SEAGOON** | (*high voice*) Yes. |
| **MORIARTY** | My little darling, marry me! Ow ow! |
| **SEAGOON** | Stop that! You'll go blind. Get him off – helppppp! |
| *FX* | *Footsteps running away, getting faster and faster* |
| **WALLACE** | By midnight Seagoon shook off Moriarty. |
| **MORIARTY** | Thank you. |
| **SEAGOON** | And the next part is the part where I say – tomorrow we sail for India. |
| *FX* | *Ship's hooter* |
| **JIM SPRIGGS** | Oh! And that's where you'll meet the great military mountaineer, Major Bloodnok. |
| *ORCHESTRA* | *Dramatic chords* |
| *FX* | *Gunfire, explosions* |

**BLOODNOK**   Oh dear – !!!

**SEAGOON**   You there!

**BLOODNOK**   Gad, look.

**SEAGOON**   Major Bloodnok?

**BLOODNOK**   The same. Late of the 3rd Heavy Herpes.

**SEAGOON**   This is the famous Eccles, late of the human race.

**BLOODNOK**   Eccles? Gad, it must be thirty years since we met.

**ECCLES**   I never met you before.

**BLOODNOK**   Then it must be longer!

▶ ▶ ▶ ▶ ▶ ▶ ▶ ▶ ▶ ▶ ▶ ▶ ▶ ▶

**ECCLES**     I wish mine was longer.

**BLOODNOK**     Of course. Well, now you're here, let me help you. Singhiz, take this gentleman's things and put them in the wicker basket marked Lot 23, 8 shillings o.n.o.

**SEAGOON**     Under the circumstances I'll be forced to stay with you.

**BLOODNOK**     Why?

**SEAGOON**     I'm skint.

**BLOODNOK**     Ah. Well, before you turn in, would you care for a nightcap?

**SEAGOON**     Yes.

**BLOODNOK**     Good – here's one with a chin strap, Now, how about a double brandy?

**SEAGOON**     Ah, no.

**BLOODNOK**     Rum?

**SEAGOON**     No.

**BLOODNOK**     Gin, then?

**SEAGOON**     Er – no.

**BLOODNOK**     Good heavens, man, haven't you got anything at all?

**SEAGOON**     I brought you this long thin green thing with several lumps held on by a bootlace tied round.

**BLOODNOK**     But I've already got one!

SEAGOON    How was I to know?

BLOODNOK   Isn't it obvious? You could have written!

SEAGOON    Would you mind holding this mangle? Thank you. Now, I'm here to offer you employment.

BLOODNOK   Work? Aaagh! (*Faints*)

FX         *Body and mangle hit floor*

SEAGOON    I got Bloodnok and the mangle onto his bed and revived hime with a glass of Footo the Wonder Boot Exploder.

FX         *Explosion – then another louder explosion*

BLOODNOK   Oh, that's better!

SEAGOON    Quick! Open the windows!

BLOODNOK   Now, tell me all –

SEAGOON    It's about klimbing Mount Everest from the inside ... (*fade*).

BLOODNOK   Klimbing, eh?

BOTH       (*ad lib, walking away*)

FX         *Construction work. Digging. Slaves singing work songs*

WALLACE    Work was begun on boring a hole up the middle of Everest.

BLOODNOK   Look at them – working like niggers!

SEAGOON    Bloodnok! That word is verboten.

**BLOODNOK**   Look at 'em – working like verbotens. Now, surprise!

**SEAGOON**   What's this huge brown paper parcel?

**BLOODNOK**   A surprise from Blighty. It's a lift.

**SEAGOON**   A lift?

**BLOODNOK**   Yes, I'm going to have it built in to Mount Everest. Seagoon, you're going to travel up in style and comfort, lad. Let's unwrap it.

**SEAGOON**   I'm the strongest, I'll tear off the paper.

**BLOODNOK**   Nothing like tearing 'em off.

**FX**   *Tearing paper – ripping noises*

**BLOODNOK**   There we are. Now let's see what it's like inside.

**FX**   *Lift door opens*

**MINNIE**   Oh, thank heaven. Is this ladies' lingerie?

**BLOODNOK**   No, it's wogs galore and loin cloths. Wait! Is it – it's Minnie Bannister! Minnie Bannister, the darling of Roper's Light Horse and the 3rd Foot and Mouth.

**MINNIE**   The same.

**BLOODNOK**   Oh, fair dear little creature. Don't you recognise me?

**MINNIE**   Dennis – Dennis Bloodnok! Were the tests clear?

**BLOODNOK**   Oh my treasure, you little beauty. (*Kissing hand*) Your little hand – let me take your ring off so I can kiss it. (*Kisses*)

| | |
|---|---|
| **MINNIE** | Oooh-ooh. |
| **BLOODNOK** | Remember Poona – the Governor's balls in 1927? |
| **MINNIE** | I'll never forget them. |
| **BLOODNOK** | What was that waltz? |
| **BLOODNOK & MINNIE** | *(sing)* 'I was born in Vienna, Where the girls and the men are, So exceedingly all bright and gay, and I blow away. . .' *(They fade away)* |
| **SEAGOON** | With eyes closed they danced in ecstasy . . . over a cliff. |
| **BLOODNOK & MINNIE** | *(sing their way back)* |
| **SEAGOON** | And back again. |
| **BLOODNOK** | Greenslade, take Madame Bannister to my tent. |
| **WALLACE** | Yes. |
| **BLOODNOK** | Not much of a part. There she goes, sweet Min Bann. She looks exactly the same as when I first met her – bloody terrible. |
| **FX** | *Whistle* |
| **BLOODNOK** | Offside! Everyone back to their own beds. |
| **FX** | *Footsteps running away* |
| **SEAGOON** | You fool, Bloodnok, that's the danger whistle. The men are going to start blasting. |
| **BLOODNOK** | Rude words cannot hurt me, lad. |

▶ ▶ ▶ ▶ ▶ ▶ ▶ ▶ ▶ ▶ ▶ ▶ ▶ ▶ ▶

SEAGOON    I'd better check that everyone has taken cover. Bluebottle?

FX    *Approaching running footsteps*

BLUEBOTTLE    I heard you call, I am coming, my Captain. I was over there eating my jelly babies in private – you get more that way.

SEAGOON    Bluebottle, run in the tunnel and see if all the men are out.

BLUEBOTTLE    Your wish is my command. I will do that, Captain. I'm not afraid. I will. (*Pause*) I say, Captain – there's a dirty big stick of dynamite in there.

SEAGOON    You're perfectly safe – it's a long fuse.

BLUEBOTTLE    I knew it would be safe. I trust my Captain. He always tells me the truth. (*Pause*) You are telling the truth – aren't you?

Spike Milligan

| | |
|---|---|
| **SEAGOON** | Yes – off you go. |
| *FX* | *Footsteps running away* |
| **SEAGOON** | There he goes, brave, tall, straight as a hockey stick and twice as thin. Even as I speak he enters the dreaded tunnel. |
| **BLUEBOTTLE** | Hello? (*Echo*) Hello, everybody. Is anybody in there? Is anyone still in the tunnel? If so, you must leave. You have ten minutes before the dynamite – |
| *FX* | *Colossal explosion – falling bits, knife, fork, spoon, marbles etc.* |
| **BLUEBOTTLE** | You rotten swine, you! You've shredded my best trousers and melted my Milky Way. Ahhh! |
| **SEAGOON** | Quick, Ellington, the coup de grâce! |
| **QUARTET** | *Music* |
| **BLOODNOK** | That night my mangle and I were so excited I didn't feel tired, so I slept with my eyes open. When I awoke, my eyes were closed. So I must have dozed off when I was asleep with my eyes shut open. Eh? |
| **SEAGOON** | You have an unsound mind. |
| **BLOODNOK** | Unsound? Hit it with this hammer. |
| *FX* | *Hammer. Wallop – loud bonggg* |
| **BLOODNOK** | Dinner is served |
| **SEAGOON** | Just hold this mangle. |
| **ECCLES** | Hello – I tought I heard der sound of a mind. |

**BLOODNOK**  Eccles, why do people take an instant dislike to me?

**ECCLES**  It saves time!

**BLOODNOK**  Just hold this mangle.

**BEARER**  Excuse me, camel's waiting to take us to foot Mount Everest.

**ECCLES**  The foot? I didn't know Everest had a foot?

**BLOODNOK**  Yes – it's got more – see here, Everest 29,000 feet.

**ECCLES**  That's a centipede.

**BLOODNOK**  Well, it had to go some where. Now, Seagoon, could you oblige me? Say, five pounds?

**SEAGOON**  Say five pounds? Right – five pounds!

**BLOODNOK**  Thank you!

**SEAGOON**  Have **you** five pounds, Eccles?

**ECCLES**  No. Have you got five pounds, Major?

**BLOODNOK**  Well, you look like a sporting man. There.

**ECCLES**  Ah. There, Neddy.

**SEAGOON**  Thanks. Here you are, Bloodnok.

**BLOODNOK**  Oh, thank you.

**ECCLES**  Just hold this mangle.

**ORCHESTRA**  *Corny music hall chord*

**WALLACE**   That appears to be the end of that corny routine. Now, the sound of camels.

*FX*   *Camels. Strange rumbling sounds – raspberries*

**SEAGOON**   We rode in silence, save for the odd noises camels are wont to make – or was it Bloodnok?

*FX*   *Explosion*

**BLOODNOK**   Oh, that curry! It was hell back there, I tell you.

**SEAGOON**   (*laughing*) It's hell back here!

**WALLACE**   Didn't you finally arrive at the mountain and find the lift installed and get in it?

**SEAGOON**   You can tell we're getting near the end.

**JIM SPRIGGS**   All get in the elevator. Going up.

*FX*   *Elevator ascending*

**BLOODNOK**   Fancy – the first men to go up Everest from the inside. Just hold this mangle.

*FX*   *Elevator*

**JIM SPRIGGS**   Three thousand feet.

*FX*   *Elevator*

**JIM SPRIGGS**   Four thousand feet

*FX*   *Elevator. Long, long pause*

**SEAGOON**   Look, this is terribly boring for the listeners.

**BLOODNOK**   Yes! But what can one do in a lift?

**JIM SPRIGGS**  You can hold this mangle.

**SEAGOON**  Spriggs, sing them a song.

**JIM SPRIGGS**  All right.

**FX**  *Long piano introduction*

**JIM SPRIGGS**  (*starts to sing*) I –

**BLOODNOK**  It's all right, we're here now!

**SEAGOON**  Hand me the flag. I claim this Union Jack for England! Well, what do you think, Bloodnok?

**BLOODNOK**  Hardly worth it for the view. Hold this mangle. (*Long pause*)

**WALLACE**  Good God – they've finished.

Announcer Wallace Greenslade to the fore

Jack Oakley

◆ ◆ ◆ ◆ ◆ ◆ ◆ ◆ ◆ ◆ ◆ ◆ ◆ ◆

# THE SILENT BUGLER

The Goon Show: 'Vintage Goons', No. 10
Recorded 23rd February, 1958
First Transmission 29th December, 1986 (Radio 4)

# Cast (main characters)

**Spike Milligan**
    'M'
    Sergeant Eccles
    Minnie Bannister

**Peter Sellers**
    Vanderschmidt
    Ticket Collector
    Colonel Brollicks
    Henry Crun
    Major Bloodnok
    Bluebottle

**Harry Secombe**
    Captain Hairy Seagoon (Agent X2)

**Ray Ellington**
    Airline official
    Russian

With The Ray Ellington Quartet, Max Geldray, and the Orchestra
conducted by Wally Stott.
Script by Spike Milligan.
Announcer Wallace Greenslade.
Producer Charles Chilton.

◆ ◆ ◆ ◆ ◆ ◆ ◆ ◆ ◆ ◆ ◆ ◆ ◆

Armed with a rubber dagger and a set of disguises that includes a ginger thermal beard, reversible plastic socks, and false cardboard skis, Agent X2 (alias Captain Hairy Seagoon) sets off on the trail of a Russian master spy (alias The Silent Bugler). However, despite such technologically advanced accessories, it is Bloodnok's plain old-fashioned undergarments which finally save our hero from a death worse than fate . . .

**WALLACE** The BBC presents Agents Sellers, Secombe and Milligan in the – er – the – er – (*Whispers*) Look, I'm new here . . .

**SECOMBE** *(whispers)* Here – on this paper . . .

**WALLACE** The Goat Show. (*Whispers*) You sure this is right?

**SECOMBE** We'll have to get another typist – it's really The Goon Show and –

*ORCHESTRA* *Awful chord*

**WALLACE** This is getting silly. Ahem – today, in the American Senate, Senator Vanderschmidt said –

**VANDERSCHMIDT** (*powerful American accent*) Money!

**WALLACE** And he continued by saying –

**VANDERSCHMIDT** Hearn. Hearn. Hearn. (*Fades*) Money – hearn hearn – money.

**WALLACE** In response on March 3rd in the House of Commons at four o'clock, the Prime Minister said –

**PM** Tea?

| | |
|---|---|
| **FX** | *Mad rush of politicians stampeding for canteen – cries of TEA! TEA! CAKE! CAKE!* |
| **WALLACE** | These ev – (*he is interrupted by the orchestra*) |
| **ORCHESTRA** | *Terrible chord* |
| **WALLACE** | These everyday exchanges in our political circles are made known to us all by the daily newspoppers – tsk tsk. But what of the secret services? |
| **SPIKE** | Yes indeed, what of them? (*Embarrassing pause*) |
| **WALLACE** | Oh, I didn't know you'd finished – it's got engaged on the door. We give you now only one story of only one minute fragment in this mosaic of political intrigue. Take the case of Agent X2. (*Fade*) |
| **SEAGOON** | I am X2. My miss – (*He is interrupted by the orchestra*) |
| **ORCHESTRA** | *Dramatic chord* |
| **SEAGOON** | For God's sake! My mission started when I was called to HQ M15. I was disguised as a commuter, but I'd hardly got on board the train when I had the uneasy feeling I was being followed – a man in uniform – |
| **FX** | *Train door slides open* |
| **SEAGOON** | He approached me with something in his hand. |
| **COLLECTOR** | Tickets, please. |
| **SEAGOON** | Oh yes! |
| **COLLECTOR** | This is a platform ticket. |

◆ ◆ ◆ ◆ ◆ ◆ ◆ ◆ ◆ ◆ ◆ ◆

**SEAGOON**     That's right, I always travel by platform.

**COLLECTOR**   Where's your ticket?

**SEAGOON**     Just joking. Here we are.

**COLLECTOR**   I know we're here, but where's your ticket?

**SEAGOON**     There.

**COLLECTOR**   Wait a minute, this ticket's from Dover to Melbourne, Steerage Class – this is the Central Line Tube.

**SEAGOON**     April Fool!

| | |
|---|---|
| **COLLECTOR** | This is December! |
| **SEAGOON** | Oh, my calendar must be slow. There. My ticket. |
| **COLLECTOR** | This ticket was issued in 1902. |
| **SEAGOON** | Really? Gad, we're running late. |
| **COLLECTOR** | And it's for the Brighton to London stagecoach. |
| **SEAGOON** | Yes, indeed. |
| **COLLECTOR** | This ain't a bloody stagecoach, mate. |
| **SEAGOON** | You mean this train isn't horsedrawn? I demand my money back. |
| **COLLECTOR** | You **got** to **pay** for the **ticket.** Where did you get on? |
| **SEAGOON** | (*aside*) Curse! The game's up. (*Aloud*) Where was that last station? |
| **COLLECTOR** | Clapham Junction. |
| **SEAGOON** | That's it. That's where I got on. |
| **COLLECTOR** | We didn't stop there. |
| **SEAGOON** | You think it was easy? |
| **COLLECTOR** | Where are you going to? |
| **SEAGOON** | The next station. |
| **COLLECTOR** | Right, that'll be eighteen shillings and threepence. |
| *FX* | *Coins – cascades of them* |

◆ ◆ ◆ ◆ ◆ ◆ ◆ ◆ ◆ ◆ ◆ ◆

**SEAGOON**  Sorry, it's all in farthings.

**COLLECTOR**  Thank you.

*FX*  *Door closes*

**SEAGOON**  Fool. Little does he know that the real fare is not eighteen and threepence, but thirty-two pounds six shillings.

**COLLECTOR**  Little does he know that I'm nothing to do with the railway at all.

*ORCHESTRA*  *Boom-boom chord*

**WALLACE**  Thus Seagoon arrived at HQ M15, with the wind behind him.

*FX*  *Raspberry. Door opens*

**'M'**  *(upper class twit)* Ah, come in X2. Now, you **know** what we want you for.

A Twit

THE LOST GOON SHOWS

| | |
|---|---|
| **SEAGOON** | No. |
| **'M'** | Oh dear. Well, don't go away. We'll think of **something.** Ever been to Russia? |
| **SEAGOON** | No – but I've been to Scunthorpe. |
| **'M'** | That'll do. Colonel Brollicks, will you explain to him? |
| **BROLLICKS** | Yes, well, we have reason to believe that the Russians have perfected a time machine. With it they could go forward into the future; once there they'd build planes that would travel faster than the speed of light. They've **got** to be stopped doing such a thing. You're the man for the job. |
| **SEAGOON** | Oh, ta! |
| **BROLLICKS** | Thank you. Are you married? |
| **SEAGOON** | No, sir. I want to remain celibate. |
| **BROLLICKS** | Understandable. Then marry a nun. Now, I would go on this mission myself, but, well, it's too dangerous. |
| **SEAGOON** | You mean, I might get killed? |
| **BROLLICKS** | Let me put it this way – yes. |
| *FX* | *Door opens* |
| **'M'** | Ah, Mr Crun! Mr – |
| **CRUN** | Ahhh – Go – go – good mor – mor – mor – morning. |

| | |
|---|---|
| **'M'** | Morning. This man hiding under the table is X2. Would you go under and brief him? |
| **CRUN** | Ah! Go – go – good mor – mor – morning, Mi – Mi – Mister – Mister – |
| **SEAGOON** | Mister Captain Hairy Seagoon at your service, sir. |
| **CRUN** | Ah yes, Mister Captain Seagoonatyourservicesir. Now, here is a photo of the Russian master spy, Igor Blimey. He's escaped from every prison camp in Europe. |
| **SEAGOON** | There's nothing on this photograph. |
| **CRUN** | He's escaped again! They call him, the Silent Bugler. |
| **SEAGOON** | The **Silent** Bugler? |
| **CRUN** | Nobody has ever seen him. But here is a rare record of him. |
| *FX* | *Record goes on – no sound, only surface hiss* |
| **SEAGOON** | I can't hear anything. |
| **CRUN** | That's him! The Silent Bugler. If you ever hear anything like **that**, be on your guard. |
| **SEAGOON** | With that warning ringing in my teeth, I spent the next three weeks training to listen to silences under Major Bloodnok. |
| *ORCHESTRA* | *'Bloodnok Theme'* |
| *FX* | *Explosions* |

**BLOODNOK**   Aah, ooh! Batman? A clean pair and hurry! Now, you were saying, Mister Captain Seagoonatyourservice?

**SEAGOON**   I said, during the last war they say you were taken prisoner.

**BLOODNOK**   Yes, yes, but I escaped.

**SEAGOON**   Where from?

**BLOODNOK**   Dartmoor. Now, first of all your disguises. Stand by to check. One ginger thermal beard with detachable bells and suppositories.

**SEAGOON**   Yes.

**BLOODNOK**   One pair of reversible plastic socks easily convertible to dog cardigan or bust of Marilyn Monroe.

**SEAGOON**   Yes

**BLOODNOK**   One pair of false cardboard skis. One fur-lined wicker teapot with underwater escape apparatus and view of the Matterhorn.

**SEAGOON**   Yes.

**BLOODNOK**   One rubber dagger.

**SEAGOON**   What's the use of a rubber dagger?

◆ ◆ ◆ ◆ ◆ ◆ ◆ ◆ ◆ ◆ ◆

**BLOODNOK**   We don't want to shed blood needlessly. Now, finance. Three thousand lire in rupees, payable in pesetas at any Mongolian bank whilst wearing tennis shoes in a thunderstorm during an equinox of the moon.

**SEAGOON**   That'll do nicely.

**BLOODNOK**   Now, the sensitivity test. I shall just blindfold you. Now, I want you to tell me what I'm doing. Right?

**SEAGOON**   Er, you're taking my gold ring off my finger.

**BLOODNOK**   Yes, yes, yes.

**SEAGOON**   Now you're removing my gold watch. And my fountain pen from my pocket.

**BLOODNOK**   Bravo, keep it up.

**SEAGOON**   Now you're taking my wallet. And my money belt – now you're tying me to a chair –

**BLOODNOK**   (*from distance*) Keep going.

**SEAGOON**   I can't feel you doing anything now. Hello, Major? Major? Hello – Hello – . . . you **SWINE!**

*ORCHESTRA*   *Awful chords again*

**WALLACE**   That appears to be the end of The Silent Bugler, Part One. Now a smile, a harmonica, a large nose – Max Geldray.

*MAX AND*   *Music*
*ORCHESTRA*

*WALLACE*   Now, the Si –

*ORCHESTRA*   *Awful chords*

**WALLACE**   The Silent Bugler, Part Two? How time flies. First, for listeners who have just tuned in, here is a rapid synopsis.

*FX*   *Run first part of show at high speed, slow down to hear Seagoon say 'you SWINE!'*

**WALLACE**   Now read on.

**SEAGOON**     Before my departure for Russia, I took one final test.

**BROLLICKS**   We want you to identify objects that will be held up in
                rapid succession. Sergeant Eccles, do your duty.

**ECCLES**      OK. The first object I hold up is **this.**

**SEAGOON**     It's a banana!

**ECCLES**      Good, good. (*Eats it*) Dat got rid of that. Now then,
                what's this?

**SEAGOON**     A pencil.

*FX*            *Sound of man eating pencil*

**ECCLES**      Good. (*Gulps*) And dat got rid of dat! What's this (*grunting
                and straining*) that I'm holding?

**SEAGOON**     Er, let me see . . .

**ECCLES**      Hurry up – I can't hold it up all day! **Come on!** Look at
                the shape.

*FX*            *Creaking noises as of something about to give way*

**SEAGOON**     Yes. I've seen one like it. Er – no, I'm not quite sure. I
                give up. What is it?

**ECCLES**      It's an elephant.

|  |  |
|---|---|
| *FX* | *Eccles drops elephant* |

**SEAGOON**    Ah, of course – he was the big one.

**ECCLES**    Ohh. I didn't know he had a big one.

**BROLLICKS**    Now, Seagoon, just one more small thing. Private Bluebottle.

**BLUEBOTTLE**    Sir! I heard you call, sir Captain, I heard you. Hello, everybody and sir. Like a jelly baby?

**BROLLICKS**    No thank you, baby.

**SEAGOON**    I understand you have a secret weapon for me.

**BLUEBOTTLE**    I have it, I have. Unscrews false kneecap, takes out secret gun. Am in agony, as I have not got false kneecap. Puts on bold face. It still hurts, though.

**SEAGOON**    Oh, what is it?

**BLUEBOTTLE**    It is my backshot pistol.

**SEAGOON**    You mean, whoever fires the pistol gets killed himself?

**BLUEBOTTLE**    Yes. You just give it to the enemy, he aims at you, and then – bang! – he gets deaded himself! He he he!

**SEAGOON**    How does it work?

▶◆◆◆◆◆◆◆◆◆◆◆◆

**BLUEBOTTLE**  I'll show you. I just point the gun at you, then I pull the trigger and – ah hah! No! **You** point it at **me,** and **you** pull the trigger.

**SEAGOON**  So. I point it at you like this.

**BLUEBOTTLE**  **No!** Don't point it at **me,** point it at **yourself** – I think –

**SEAGOON**  But you said –

*FX*  *Gunshot*

**BLUEBOTTLE**  *(screams)* You rotten swine you – right in my hat, look at the hole! People can see in now and laugh at my school hair cut! *(Seagoon and Bluebottle walk away, Seagoon comforting him)*
*(Silence)*

**WALLACE**  Oh! The Silent Bugler, Part Three. Sorry, took me by suprise.

**PETER**  In a dark car wearing a frilly hat with the brim well over the headlights, Seagoon was driven to a submerged airport.

*FX*  *Plane on tarmac, engine running*

**WALLACE**  *(announcing through bull horn)* Will all passengers with a disguised M15 ticket for mystery flight X to undisclosed destination, please inflate their false wigs and crawl as inconspicuously as possible to the isolated black plane standing in the shadow of the barbed wire. Thank you.

**OFFICIAL**   Mystery flight X, this way, please. Passports, please. Name?

**BLOODNOK**   Mrs Gladys Murgatroyd, widow and go go dancer with walnuts.

**OFFICIAL**   Right, next.

**ECCLES**   Woof woof, growl, woof.

*FX*   *Stamping passport*

**OFFICIAL**   Right, next.

Spike Milligan

**WALLACE**   Just an old BBC announcer.

**OFFICIAL**   Good luck. Next.

*FX*   *Rubber stamp*

**PETER**   Sir Arthur Brogglers, child molester and plumber.

*FX*   *Rubber stamp*

**OFFICIAL**   (*screams*) Oh! my finger!!!

**PETER**   Little does he know I am not Sir Arthur Brogglers child molester and plumber but – Dick Scratcher.

**ECCLES**   Little does he know that I am not woof woof, growl, but growl, woof woof.

**BLOODNOK**   Little do they know that I am not Mrs Gladys Murgatroyd, widow and go go dancer, but Secret Agent X.

**OFFICIAL**   Now you, sir?

**SEAGOON**   I am X2, or Captain Hairy Seagoon. Secret British agent.

**OFFICIAL**   Ha ha ha! You – **you** a secret agent? (*Reels away in fits of laughter*)

**SEAGOON**   Plainly he didn't believe me.

**OFFICIAL**   Close bulkhead doors. Fasten your safety belts, please.

**MINNIE**   Morning.

**OMNES**   Morning.

*FX*   *Plane starts to move away*

**MINNIE**   Morning, everybody. Everybody take your seats please.
All safety belts to be fastened. Come, Captain Seagoon,
you **must** fasten your belt now.

**SEAGOON**   Why?

**MINNIE**   Your trousers are coming down. Now, don't be nervous,
flying isn't dangerous – **crashing** is dangerous.

*FX*   *Plane takes off*

**QUARTET**   Music

**SEAGOON**   By now I was deep in enemy territory. Very very deep. I
was dropped without a parachute. Walking along the
Fredstrasse in Dresden I was halted by two men heavily
disguised as Englishmen.

**BLOODNOK**   Good morgen, Herr Seagoon. And how is mein herr this
morning?

**SEAGOON**   Going a bit thin on top.

◆ ◆ ◆ ◆ ◆ ◆ ◆ ◆ ◆ ◆ ◆ ◆

**BLOODNOK**  Achtung, Spitfire, egg in the eye, Rommel, gezeitung, up the old gelingen blar . . .

**SEAGOON**  (*aside*) I **must** reply. Ahem. Si si signor. (*Aside*) Poor German fool. Little do they know that I am **not** really a German, but I speak the language fluently.

**BLOODNOK**  Poor German fool. Little does he know that I am not a poor German fool, but Major Bloodnok, a poor English fool.

**ECCLES**  Pardon, mein herr, gute morgen . . .

**FX**  *Austrian cuckoo clock*

**SEAGOON**  Ach, Himmel! Ten to one – time to open my sealed orders.

**BLOODNOK**  Two twenty – time to open my sealed orders.

**ECCLES**  Twenty to three – time to open my sealed orders.

**SEAGOON**  It says, The man standing before you is Major Bloodnok X.

**BLOODNOK**  Mine says, The man standing before you is Captain Seagoon X2, who has just been informed who **you** are.

**ECCLES**  Mine says, Beat two eggs, add four ounces of flour . . . Ooh, it's Mrs Beeton's Cookery Book.

**BLOODNOK**    X2?

**SEAGOON**    X?

**ECCLES**    Er – two x and bacon!

**BLOODNOK**    We shall meet here when the clock strikes one.

**SEAGOON**    Right.

**FX**    *Clock strikes one*

**SEAGOON**    Bloodnok!

**BLOODNOK**    Seagoon!

**ECCLES**    Two x and bacon

**FX**    *Bloodnok and Seagoon hitting Eccles*

**BLOODNOK**    That's enough, we'll save him for later.

**FX**    *Phone rings*

**BLOODNOK**    Don't answer that phone! It's ringing in Russian!

**SEAGOON**    Don't worry, I'll put on this false thermal beard. Now. Hello? Who's speaking?

**WALLACE**    If you take that bloody silly beard off, I'll tell you. Now listen, this is HQ M15. Orders. The location of the time machine is in the Dresden Opera House.

**ECCLES**    I can't sing a note.

**SEAGOON**    Shut up! Men, the Dresden Opera House, hurry.

◆ ◆ ◆ ◆ ◆ ◆ ◆ ◆ ◆ ◆ ◆ ◆

**FX**    *Men streaking away – fade out then fade back*

**BLOODNOK**    (*breathless*) Ah, here we are – exhausted. What's this say? Today's symphony concert featuring – *Relgub Tneliseht?*

**SEAGOON**    Gad, that spells the Silent Bugler backwards.

**FX**    *Orchestra tuning up*

**ECCLES**    Ah, here's an empty box. Not a match left in it.

**BLOODNOK**    We're just in time to miss the first movements.

**SEAGOON**    Look at the orchestra. They must be all of a hundred and fifty.

**ECCLES**    Some look much younger.

BBC

| | |
|---|---|
| **SEAGOON** | Shut up, and listen. |
| *GRAMS* | *Opening of 'Unfinished Symphony'* |
| **SEAGOON** | I wonder which one is the Silent Bugler. |
| **BLOODNOK** | That's him. Curse, he's stopped playing. |
| **SEAGOON** | I didn't hear him. |
| **BLOODNOK** | Well, listen – there he is now. |
| **SEAGOON** | Where, where? |
| **BLOODNOK** | Blast, he's gone again. |
| **SEAGOON** | What was that? The music seemed to repeat. |
| **BLOODNOK** | I didn't notice anything, and I know my Wagner backwards. |
| **SEAGOON** | They're not playing it backwards. |
| *GRAMS* | *Music slows down like a gramophone record winding down* |
| **SEAGOON** | Good heavens, the orchestra's **miming** to a gramophone record – another BBC economy! |
| **BLOODNOK** | Then the Silent Bugler – |
| **SEAGOON** | He doesn't exist – it must be all a bluff. |
| **BLOODNOK** | You mean – |
| **SEAGOON** | The whole orchestra are secret Russian agents. We must get out of here quick. |
| **ECCLES** | But the time machine? |

**SEAGOON**   We must split up.

**ECCLES**   How do I split up?

**SEAGOON**   Shut up! We must split up and search under the theatre. Wait – (*slowly*) – how do I know you're both not enemy agents? Your identity cards, please.

**BLOODNOK**   My card.

**SEAGOON**   (*reads*) Major D. Bloodnok. My card.

**BLOODNOK**   (*reads*) Captain H. Seagoon.

**ECCLES**   My card!

**BLOODNOK**   (*reads*) The two of clubs.

**FX**   *Eccles being hit*

**WALLACE**   Here is a short résumé of what you're missing on TV:

**PETER**   Helen Lovejoy, beautiful heiress to the Halibut millions, has been jilted at the altar by Villion de Paprikon, one legged son of Louis XIV. Peter, Villion's Eton boating friend has heard this, but being in Tibet not as loud, and he has embarrassed Mary, his fiancée, who being the only cousin of Sir Ray Ellington has caught it off Dick Scratcher and has passed the title on to Baron Geldray, also heir to the Halibut oil millions.

**WALLACE**   Have you finished?

**FX**   *Voices echo from now on*

**BLOODNOK**   We are alone under the theatre.

Jockey by
Peter

| | |
|---|---|
| **SEAGOON** | Look! The time machine. |
| **ECCLES** | It says half past four. |
| **SEAGOON** | Shut up! |
| **BLOODNOK** | I'll just put this bomb under it – stand back – |
| *FX* | *Immediate explosion* |
| **BLOODNOK** | Could have done with a longer fuse. |
| **ECCLES** | Is dat why we're up in the air? |
| **SEAGOON** | Somebody's coming! |
| **RUSSIAN** | Come down from up there! Hands up in Russian! |
| **BLOODNOK** | The KGB! Run for it in English. |
| *FX* | *Footsteps running away followed by bullets whizzing past* |

◆ ◆ ◆ ◆ ◆ ◆ ◆ ◆ ◆ ◆ ◆ ◆ ◆

| | |
|---|---|
| **SEAGOON** | Taxi! |
| *FX* | *Taxi screeches to a halt — then races off. Fast car. Horses. Train. Jet plane. Bus. Screeching brakes.* |
| **ECCLES** | We've made it. |
| **SEAGOON** | Safe at last. |
| **RUSSIAN** | So, you all came back. Hands up in Russian again. Up, down. Up, down. When we take prisoners we like them fit! |
| **BLOODNOK** | Too late, Ruskie — we destroyed your time machine. We can die knowing we've done our job. |
| **ECCLES** | Wot you mean, **we**? |
| **SEAGOON** | Shut up! |
| **RUSSIAN** | You fools! |
| **ECCLES** | Tell us something new. |
| **RUSSIAN** | You only destroyed a replica of the time machine. |
| **SEAGOON** | Curse. Foiled by an unpatriotic script. |
| **BLOODNOK** | (*whispers*) Wait. I happen to be wearing red flannel underdrawers. If I could lower my trousers, he'll salute! |
| **SEAGOON** | I'll pull from the back. One, two, three. |
| *FX* | *Ripping material* |
| **RUSSIAN** | Ah — I salute our glorious flag. Long live Russia! |

◆ ◆ ◆ ◆ ◆ ◆ ◆ ◆ ◆ ◆ ◆ ◆

**BLOODNOK**     Get him!

**SEAGOON**     OK Ruskie, hands up, down, up, down – knees bend, bend – stretch, on the spot running – begin!

**RUSSIAN**     (*gasping*) Don't shoot. I tell you where time machine is – page 33!

*FX*     *Rapid turning of pages*

**SEAGOON**     Right. No mistakes this time. Put this bomb under it – it's timed to go off on the 23rd November.

**BLOODNOK**     That's my birthday!

**SEAGOON and ECCLES**     (*sing*) Happy birthday to –

*FX*     *Explosion. Disappearing screams as our heroes are blown up*

**WALLACE**     Well, that's that – will the last person out please lock up.

*ORCHESTRA*     *Awful chords*

◆ ◆ ◆ ◆ ◆ ◆ ◆ ◆ ◆ ◆ ◆ ◆

Jack Oakley

*Ray Ellington sings, Max Geldray (left) watches*

BBC

# THE DREADED PIANO CLUBBER

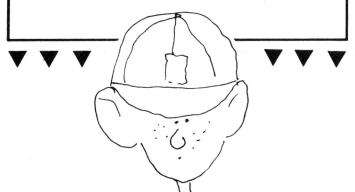

The Goon Show: 'Vintage Goons', No. 12
Recorded 9th March, 1958
First Transmission Boxing Day, 1986 (Radio 4)

# Cast (main characters)

**Spike Milligan**
>   Dudley Pringe
>   Sergeant
>   Minnie Bannister
>   Eccles
>   Count Moriarty

**Peter Sellers**
>   Henry Crun
>   Captain Bluebottle
>   William Cobblers
>   Churchill
>   Grytpype

**Harry Secombe**
>   Constable Ned Seagoon

**Wallace Greenslade**
>   The Judge

With The Ray Ellington Quartet, Max Geldray, and the Orchestra
conducted by Wally Stott.
Script by Spike Milligan.
Announcer Wallace Greenslade.
Producer Charles Chilton.

It was a foggy winter's night when the Piano Clubber struck down his first innocent victim, a Mr Henry Crun. Young Constable Ned Seagoon of the River Police was quickly on the scene, but it was not until some fifty years later that he at last tracked down the elusive Clubber, and faced his quarry in a final showdown . . .

WALLACE  In an endeavour to prove that radio is not blind we present after a successful season at Rowton House, another programme in the series, which by careful planning, meticulous writing and superb presentation has managed to avoid winning the Radio Award. Peter Sellers, Harry Secombe and Spike Milligan in –

HARRY  It's my turn – ahem. The Goon Show.

*FX*  *Very badly played, out-of-tune piano during which it falls to pieces*

PRINGE  Good evening. My name is Dudley Pringe, contemporary armchair detective and trainee plumber. Tonight from my case book I'd like to tell you the story of a krim that shook England. To tell you more is a man who remembers it all.

HARRY  (*upper class twit*) Thank you, Dudley, thank you. I'm **not** the man who remembers it all, so I'll step down. Thank you.

WALLACE  Thank you. Every now and again, there occurs a krim that makes us sit up, others sit down, some stand and face East – it all depends.

▼ ▼ ▼ ▼ ▼ ▼ ▼ ▼ ▼ ▼ ▼ ▼ ▼

**PRINGE**   For some time now the Goons have had access to Scotland Yard's secret files – thanks to an arrangement with the police known as Dropsy Bill, because he has dropsy.

**PETER**   (*American 'March of Time' voice*) From these confidential files comes a story that no Sunday newspaper would dare to print as it hasn't got big tits. The story of – The Dreaded Piano Clubber.

*GRAMS*   *Same awful piano accompanied by orchestra ends in argument between pianist and conductor*

*FX*   *Big Ben chimes. Fog horn. Footsteps of bobby on the beat*

**WALLACE**   On such a foggy night an English bobby walks his beat.

*FX*   *Loud 'klunk' as man walks into lamp post*

**ECCLES**   Oh –

**SEAGOON**   It was such a winter's night as this when **I**, Constable Ned Seagoon of Long Division, London River Police, joined the river police.

*FX*   *Splash as body falls in water. Wading through water*

**SEAGOON**   I'll be glad when we get a launch, Sergeant.

**SERGEANT**   It is a bit chilly on the truncheon, I must say. Still, we must guard our great river Thames.

**SEAGOON**   Yes. We'd better walk up the Embankment and get dry before we go in again.

*FX*   *Piano*

| | |
|---|---|
| **SERGEANT** | What was that noise? |
| **SEAGOON** | It sounded like a piano. I'll make a note! |
| *FX* | *One piano note* |
| **SERGEANT** | It's already made one. |
| *FX* | *Piano falling on a man. Shattering noise and groans* |
| **SEAGOON** | It came from over there – points. |
| *FX* | *Footsteps running away, then back* |
| **SEAGOON** | Look, a body in the gutter. Quick, Sergeant, take down this description. Five feet two short, tubby, wearing blue trousers and jacket, good looking. |
| **SERGEANT** | Right. |
| **SEAGOON** | That takes care of me. Now, the body. Wearing city suit, flattened bowler hat and bowler trousers. Carrying ear trumpet, side whiskers, bald. Sex, male. |
| **SERGEANT** | Search his pockets, Jim. |
| *FX* | *Jingling coins* |
| **SEAGOON** | Five pounds. |
| **SERGEANT** | Oh, thank you, sir! |
| **SEAGOON** | Not a word to the Inspector or he'll want some. |
| **SERGEANT** | The crook! |
| **SEAGOON** | Here's a birth certificate in his hip pocket. Gad, |

according to this, his hip pocket is a hundred and thirty years old. So this might not be murder after all, this man might have died from natural causes.

**SERGEANT**   I don't think he died from either, Jim.

**SEAGOON**   Why not?

**SERGEANT**   He's getting up, Jim.

**CRUN**   Aah-aaaah-aaaaah.

**SEAGOON**   Have you got all that down, Sergeant?

**SERGEANT**   Yes, sir.

**SEAGOON**   Easy, old man.

**CRUN**   Where am I?

**SEAGOON**   England, sir.

**CRUN**   England?

**OMNES**   (*sing*) 'There'll Always Be An England ...'

**SEAGOON**   What happened, sir?

**CRUN**   I fainted.

**SEAGOON**   Fainted – when?

**CRUN**   Just after a man struck me down with a piano.

**SEAGOON**   Struck – with a piano? Is that what these bits are?

**CRUN**   Some of them are mine.

▼ ▼ ▼ ▼ ▼ ▼ ▼ ▼ ▼ ▼ ▼ ▼ ▼

**SEAGOON**  A piano? Clubbed with a piano? Did you get the number of the instrument?

**CRUN**  No, he had his lights out. But I can describe the man.

**SEAGOON**  Good. Take this down.

**SERGEANT**  Right, sir.

**CRUN**  He was wearing turquoise trousers.

**SERGEANT**  How do you spell turquoise?

**SEAGOON**  I don't.

**SERGEANT**  I'll just pronounce it.

**CRUN**  A shirt, a tie, a jacket, a hat, socks, and one pair of shoes.

**SEAGOON**  Splendid. With that description, if ever he enters a nudist colony he's a gonner. Anything else?

**CRUN**  Yes, he was carrying a piano, and this recording of Max Geldray.

***MAX AND ORCHESTRA***  *Music (It ends with piano falling on him)*

***FX***  *Disintegrating piano. Screams. Police whistles*

**WALLACE**  That was the second time the Piano Clubber struck. In the months to come he struck twenty-eight times, more times than British Leyland. Each time he struck his victim with a piano. Each time he crept up on his victim from behind. And each time his victim was Henry Crun. Each time in the key of C. Public opinion demanded a public enquiry.

▼ ▼ ▼ ▼ ▼ ▼ ▼ ▼ ▼ ▼ ▼ ▼ ▼ ▼

**FX**    *Crowd — mumbles — occasional sheep — chickens. Gavel on desk*

**JUDGE**    Order, please, order. First witness.

**BLUEBOTTLE**    My name is Captain Bluebottle.

**OMNES**    Hurray! Hurray!

**BLUEBOTTLE**    Thank you, friends of Bluebottle. Now for an encore. (*Sings*) 'The girl that I marry will have to be, born some where in Finch – er – ley —'

**ORCHESTRA**    *Guitar accompaniment*

**JUDGE**    Silence. Stop that singing, and I'll stop playing this guitar.

**BLUEBOTTLE**    Fair's fair.

**JUDGE**    Your evidence?

**BLUEBOTTLE**    On the night of the attack I was walking down Bongers Lane, when suddenly I stopped.

**JUDGE**    Why?

**BLUEBOTTLE**    I must have been tired. My little tootsies were steaming after certain rock and roll dances. (*Sings*) 'One o'clock, two o'clock, 3 o'clock rock . . .'

**ORCHESTRA**    *Guitar accompaniment*

**JUDGE**    Stop singing and I'll stop playing!

**BLUEBOTTLE**    Fair's fair!

**JUDGE**    And when you stopped, you saw the victim, Mr Crun, was lying in the gutter, yes?

**BLUEBOTTLE**   When I stopped, I saw the victim, Mr Crun, was –

**JUDGE**   Look, I've said all this!

**BLUEBOTTLE**   Oh, well. Escaping over a wall was a man carrying a wooden-type piano. You didn't say that, did you?

**JUDGE**   Why, as a responsible citizen, didn't you request the man with the piano to stop?

**BLUEBOTTLE**   He wasn't playing it.

**JUDGE**   Next witness.

**FIRST CLERK**   Call William Cobblers.

**SECOND CLERK**   Call William Cobblers.

**FX**   *Footsteps approach*

**FIRST CLERK**   William Cobblers, raise your right leg and say after me: I swear –

**COBBLERS**   I swear.

**FIRST CLERK**   I also drink and smoke . . .

**COBBLERS**   I also drink and smoke.

**JUDGE**   Take the stand. Now, you've come a long way to give evidence.

**COBBLERS**   All the way from Cape Town, mate. The fare cost me every penny I had.

| JUDGE | We appreciate you making this long journey. Now, on the night of the crime, where were you? |
| COBBLERS | I was in Cape Town. |
| JUDGE | Next witness. |
| FIRST CLERK | Call Minnie Bannister! |
| SECOND CLERK | Call Minnie Bannister. |
| FAR-OFF VOICE | Call Minnie Bannister. |
| FX | *Fast running footsteps* |
| MINNIE | My name is Minnie Bannister, spinster. |
| JUDGE | What is your association with the victim, Mr Crun? |
| MINNIE | The RAC, but we've been barred. |
| JUDGE | Why? |
| MINNIE | We haven't got a car. |
| JUDGE | Are you husband and wife? |
| MINNIE | No, just wife – he does it. |
| JUDGE | Now, what are your occupations? |
| MINNIE | Henry collects foreign stamps, and I knock my knees together. |
| JUDGE | Aren't you ashamed of yourselves? |
| MINNIE | Only on Bank Holidays. |

JUDGE    Miss Bannister, after Mr Crun was first struck by this piano, was there any change in him?

MINNIE    Yes. One pound in shillings.

JUDGE    Anything else?

MINNIE    Yes, his hat was over his eyes.

JUDGE    I take it this was caused by the force of the piano landing on it?

MINNIE    No, it's too big for him.

JUDGE    And after that, did he put anything inside his hat to absorb the shock?

MINNIE    Yes.

JUDGE    What?

MINNIE    His head.

CRUN    I object. I object.

JUDGE    To what do you object, Mr Crun?

CRUN    I object to being struck on the head by a piano.

JUDGE    Objection sustained. I find no reason to continue this enquiry, as the information obtained is of a sketchy nature. We will therefore have to wait until further attacks have taken place.

CRUN    I object to further attacks!

JUDGE    Mr Crun, you want us to find the assailant?

| CRUN | Yes. |
|---|---|
| JUDGE | Then you **must** let the attacks continue. If we don't find him, he might attack you again. |
| CRUN | Next time, I shall vote Communist, I tell you. (*He fades away, objecting*) |
| FX | *Series of piano attacks on Mr Crun* |
| SEAGOON | The attacks continued at the rate of one per week. The weeks occurred at the rate of five per month. Then the piano clubber struck in a new and terrible manner. |
| CRUN | (*terror*) With the loud pedal down. |
| FX | *Extra loud piano crash, groans* |
| CRUN | (*smothered*) Helppp . . . helpp . . . |
| SEAGOON | England was horrified. The BBC gave out warnings. |
| WALLACE | The police are appealing to the public to help track down the dreaded piano clubber. If you are hit by a piano, please don't hush it up. Tell a policeman. Make sure you are never on the streets alone. It is known that he never makes his attacks **inside** a building. So if, like myself, you work indoors, you are – |
| FX | *He is struck by a piano* |
| SEAGOON | The piano clubber had struck **inside** the BBC. We decided to trap him using Ray Ellington. |
| QUARTET | *Music* |
| FX | *Piano crashes on Ray Ellington* |

▼ ▼ ▼ ▼ ▼ ▼ ▼ ▼ ▼ ▼ ▼ ▼ ▼ ▼

*The dreaded piano clubber? No, Ray Ellington*

**SEAGOON**  Yes, the dreaded piano clubber had gone racist! Under pressure, Parliament was assembled to pass new laws.

*FX*  *Crowd – mumbles, odd chicken*

**FIRST MP**  Under the circumstances, the piano has become a lethal weapon – it will have to be licensed.

**SECOND MP**  Yes, yes. Anyone caught with a piano on their person without a licence should be prosecuted.

**VOICE**  Keep them on a lead!

▼ ▼ ▼ ▼ ▼ ▼ ▼ ▼ ▼ ▼ ▼ ▼

| | |
|---|---|
| **FIRST MP** | The honourable member's suggesting that people arriving at Heathrow will have to declare their pianos? |
| **VOICE** | What about Bechsteins? |
| **SECOND MP** | Yes, he'll have to declare his as well! |
| **OLD MAN** | It's a lot of rubbish! |
| **OLDER MAN** | What is? |
| **OLD MAN** | Wandsworth Municipal tip. |
| **ALMOST DEAD MAN** | What's this got to do with pianos? |
| **OLD MAN** | Absolutely nothing |
| **ALMOST DEAD MAN** | I see. |
| **WALLACE** | That night, Churchill addressed Parliament. |
| *FX* | *Murmurs* |
| **CHURCHILL** | Anybody who is struck down by this dreaded piano clubber must be blind. A full sized piano – I ask you . . . Isn't it possible to see a man coming towards you with a . . . |
| *FX* | *Piano crash* |
| **CHURCHILL** | (*groans*) Never has so much fallen on so few – |
| *FX* | *Uproar – police sirens – police whistles* |
| **CHURCHILL** | (*very dramatic*) Get me out – save the leader of England! |

| | |
|---|---|
| **POLICEMAN** | Easy sir, over-acting doesn't help. Can I have your autograph? It's not for me, it's for my little daughter, Clem Atlee. |
| **SEAGOON** | This is terrible – |
| **ECCLES** | Yer – but I didn't write it! |
| **SEAGOON** | Even in Parliament the dreaded piano clubber has struck. |
| **WALLACE** | Then suddenly in December without warning, suddenly the violent attacks suddenly violently ceased. Suddenly, eh? |
| **CONSTABLE** | I think, Inspector, he's having the instrument retuned. |
| **WALLACE** | The police swooped on every piano tuner in London. |
| **SEAGOON** | Ah, here's another piano tuner in London, Mr Crun. |
| **CRUN** | I wonder if we shall have any luck this time. |
| *FX* | *Shop door opening, tinkling shop bell* |
| **SEAGOON** | Nobody about in the shop. Is there anyone in? |
| **CRUN** | Yes, me. |
| **SEAGOON** | Who are you? |
| **CRUN** | Mr Crun, the famous victim. I came in with you for protection. |
| **SEAGOON** | So, there's only you and me. |
| **CRUN** | In any case, whoever works in this dreadful filthy piano shop must be right off his head. |

**ECCLES**    Hello, good evening. You want to buy a piano?

**FX**    *A few plink plonks on piano*

**SEAGOON**    I'm looking for a criminal.

**ECCLES**    Oh, that's one make I haven't got.

**SEAGOON**    Don't be silly, I wouldn't trust buying a piano in this dump.

**ECCLES**    Dump! This house a dump! Famous men come here. Do you know who comes here?

**SEAGOON**    No.

**ECCLES**    Monsieur Splonson de Groyne.

**SEAGOON**    Is he famous?

**ECCLES**    No, but he comes here.

**SEAGOON**    Look, I'm from the Yard.

**ECCLES**    Oh, dat your bin outside?

**SEAGOON**    I'm looking for a person who has been using a piano with force.

**ECCLES**    Ah, Liberace!

**SEAGOON**    I must warn you that this is a case of ipso facto carborundum dominus vobiscum!

**ECCLES**    What do all them words mean?

▼  ▼  ▼  ▼  ▼  ▼  ▼  ▼  ▼  ▼  ▼  ▼  ▼

**SEAGOON**  I don't know, but they make me sound intelligent. They fooled you.

**ECCLES**  Any words fool me.

**SEAGOON**  Cat? Dog?

**ECCLES**  Yer!

**SEAGOON**  Ah well, this makes my job easier. Cat – dog – you say this is a piano shop?

**ECCLES**  OK, this is a piano shop.

**SEAGOON**  Cat – dog – explain that notice in your window. The one that says 'For Sale – African elephants, house-trained.'

**ECCLES**  I don't stock anything like that, I never have.

Croonaphant

**SEAGOON**    Supposing people saw that, came in here and asked for an elephant.

**ECCLES**    Well, I'd just say, I'm sorry sir, I haven't got one.

**SEAGOON**    But that's mad.

**ECCLES**    I know, but civility costs nothing.

**SEAGOON**    Cat – dog – do you mind if we inspect your pianos?

**ECCLES**    Go ahead, it shouldn't take long.

**SEAGOON**    Why not?

**ECCLES**    I haven't got any. Ha ha ha ha. Oh, ha ha ha ha ha. Oh –

**SEAGOON**    Hee! Hee! Good boy –

**CRUN**    He's lying! That piano – that's the one! That's the very one that struck me down.

**SEAGOON**    Are you positive?

**CRUN**    Yes. The dent in the back fits me perfectly.

**SEAGOON**    Then we've got him. I'll have a constant watch kept on that dent. As soon as he calls to collect it, it's curtains.

**ECCLES**    I don't sell curtains –

**SEAGOON**    Shut up! Silence for this music link . . .

**ORCHESTRA**    *Musical link*

**WALLACE**    So they waited. One day, two, three, a week, two weeks, a fortnight, a month, two months, a year, two years, three, ten, twenty, thirty, forty –

OMNES      *(sing)* Fifty years ago . . .

SEAGOON    Then one midnight as we watched, a night-shirted figure in hair net and curlers ran out of the piano shop.

ECCLES     Help, aaagh, help! Helpp!

SEAGOON    Steady, cat – dog – take it easy. Settle down, boy. What's happened?

ECCLES     The piano clubber's piano. It's gone. It was stolen while I was asleep.

SEAGOON    Are you sure?

ECCLES     Of course I'm sure, I was sleeping on it.

SEAGOON    What key were you sleeping in?

ECCLES     A flat.

SEAGOON    He can't be far away – the show only lasts another few minutes. Sergeant?

SERGEANT   Here, sir.

SEAGOON    I want you to head the dreaded piano clubber off. Have you got your whistle?

SERGEANT   Yes.

SEAGOON    Right. If he hits you with his piano, give a loud blast then blow your whistle.

**SERGEANT**  Supposing I get killed?

**SEAGOON**  Then give three blasts and lay in the direction of down. Is that clear?

     *FX*  *Piano clubber's signature tune*

**SEAGOON**  Did you hear that? The piano clubber's signature tune! It came from down that street.

     *FX*  *Footsteps running backwards and forwards, over which announcer explains:*

**WALLACE**  While our heroes are seeking out the piano clubber, I'd like to tell you the current BBC news. The Deputy Light Controller of Overseas Home Service Programmes has become engaged to Ethel Croll. This has caused quite a stir, as Ethel Croll is married to Fred Ponk, Outside Broadcast Engineer. It promises to be quite an interesting battle of wits. I think that these snippets of news show that the Corporation is not without its thrills. We return now to the piano clubber thing . . .

**SEAGOON**  There he is – in that alley.

**SERGEANT**  I'll get him when he plays again.

     *FX*  *Piano. Gunshots. Scream. Running footsteps*

**SERGEANT**  Got him!

**SEAGOON**  After him! Follow the trail of blood-stained notes.

   *GRAMS*  *Old fashioned silent film chase music*

**WALLACE**  The trail led them to a lonely Scots crofter's cottage in the Hilton Hotel.

▼ ▼ ▼ ▼ ▼ ▼ ▼ ▼ ▼ ▼ ▼ ▼ ▼ ▼

**CRUN**   I tell you, I don't like the look of it.

**SEAGOON**   Then don't look at it.

**CRUN**   At my age you have to look at it just to make sure it's there.

**FX**   *Thud*

**ECCLES**   Oooh! Somebody threw a stone on my head, and it hit me, **right** on the head.

**FX**   *Paper rustling*

**SEAGOON**   There's a piece of paper wrapped round it.

**CRUN**   What's he got a piece of paper wrapped round his head for?

**SEAGOON**   The **stone,** you idiot!

**CRUN**   It's got writing on it.

**SEAGOON**   What does it say?

**CRUN**   Sorry, Eccles, I meant to hit Seagoon.

**SEAGOON**   Signed, the Dreaded Piano Clubber. It came from that top window.

**MORIARTY**   (*distant*) You'll never take me alive!

**SEAGOON**   Gad, it's Count Moriarty. Come down, Moriarty! I'll blow this whistle!

**MORIARTY**   Ah, not that, not the whistle – shall I come down with my hands up or come up with my hands down?

**SEAGOON**    Yes! Eccles, keep him covered.

**ECCLES**    I'll get a blanket.

**MORIARTY**    Don't shoot, I've only one change of underwear. I'm allergic to death!

**SEAGOON**    Sergeant, put the handcuffs on.

**SERGEANT**    Don't you think they'd look better on him?

**SEAGOON**    Oh alright! Now, Moriarty! Swallow these handcuffs and confess.

**MORIARTY**    (*gulp*) I confess –

**SEAGOON**    Go on.

**MORIARTY**    I confess – I've just swallowed some handcuffs!

**GRYTPYPE**    Let **me** do the talking, Moriarty. I have the teeth.

**SEAGOON**    Exactly who are you?

**GRYTPYPE**    I'm exactly Hercules Grytpype-Thynne.

**SEAGOON**    How do you spell that?

**GRYTPYPE**    T-H-A-T. I'm his solicitor.

**MORIARTY**    Yes – he's been soliciting all night.

**GRYTPYPE**    I'm advising my client to confess and pay me five pounds.

**MORIARTY**    I confess. I am not the piano clubber!

**SEAGOON**   What? Sergeant, take me away and lock me up with these sound effects!

*FX*   *Key – chains – iron door slams*

**SEAGOON**   At last I'm safe from the piano clubber – under lock and key. Ha ha ha!

*FX*   *Piano crashes on Seagoon*

**SEAGOON**   (*muffled*) Let me out!

**WALLACE**   Pretty obvious, wasn't it!

(*Pause*)

**ECCLES**   Dog – cat – I'll master dem one day . . .

# TWO ROYAL PAGES

Spike Milligan

The Goons and Prince Charles at Peter Sellers'
home in Elstead, Surrey, in May 1968

*Prince Charles being shown how to hold Britt Ekland*

Spike Milligan

*The Goons and Prince Charles pointing to the British Empire*

Spike Milligan

Jack Oakley

# THE SIEGE OF FORT KNIGHT

The Goon Show: 'Vintage Goons', No. 13 (a.k.a. 'The Siege of Fort Night')
Recorded 16th March, 1958
First Transmission 27th December, 1986 (Radio 4)

## Cast (main characters)

**Spike Milligan**
Mate
Minnie Bannister
Chief of Biguns Tribe
Eccles

**Peter Sellers**
Army Officer
Henry Crun
Major Bloodnok
Butler
Bluebottle

**Harry Secombe**
Major Seagoon
A Welshman

**Ray Ellington**
African Customs Officer

With The Ray Ellington Quartet, Max Geldray, and the Orchestra
conducted by Wally Stott.
Script by Spike Milligan.
Announcer Wallace Greenslade.
Producer Charles Chilton.

An underwater military gas stove is all that stands between Fort Knight and annihilation at the hands of the Biguns tribe. But – can Inventor Crun construct one in time? (He can't get the wood, you know.) Can Major Seagoon get it to the fort on time? The journey is fraught with impossibilities . . . Thus unfolds this gripping saga of a Long March – long by anyone's calendar . . .

**WALLACE** For the last time this evening at popular prices, the unpopular face of capitalism – The Goon Show.

**ORCHESTRA** *Corny chords*

**SEAGOON** Presenting the Siege of Fort Knight.

**WALLACE** The scene – a lonely British outpost in a lonely British outpost.

**ARMY OFFICER** Gentlemen, as you see on this map, thirty thousand miles away deep in the liver of Africa –

**SEAGOON** You mean the heart, sir.

**ARMY OFFICER** No! This place is much further down. In the depths of the jungle and despair, the gallant British garrison at Fort Knight are hard pressed by Biguns natives –

**SEAGOON** Biguns?

**ARMY OFFICER** Yes, some have very big 'uns. Unless this garrison is relieved within **fourteen days,** Fort Knight is finished, and I feel a terrible pun coming.

**SEAGOON**  Can't they hold out for an extra week?

**ARMY OFFICER**  Rubbish. Who's heard of a fortnight lasting three weeks?

**MATE**  I have – it was in Scunthorpe

**ARMY OFFICER**  Fort Knight needs relief.

**SEAGOON**  Reinforcements?

**ARMY OFFICER**  No, no, they have all the men they require.

**SEAGOON**  Ammunition?

**ARMY OFFICER**  They've plenty!

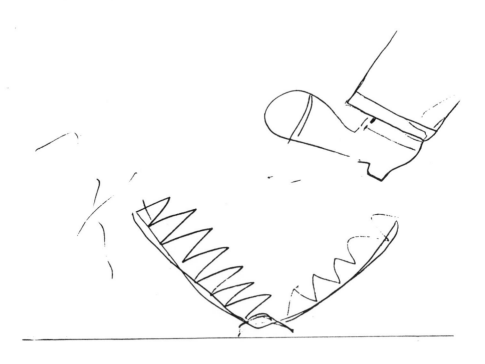

**SEAGOON**   Provisions?

**ARMY OFFICER**   They've got ample.

**SEAGOON**   They can't live on ample alone.

**ARMY OFFICER**   Worse – they've nothing to cook it on.

**SEAGOON**   Uncooked ample – you know what that means.

**MATE**   The squits!

**SEAGOON**   Yes. In a matter of days they'll be struck – no laundry will go near them.

**ARMY OFFICER**   And in forty-eight hours the monsoon will arrive.

**SEAGOON**   Bang in the middle of the rainy season.

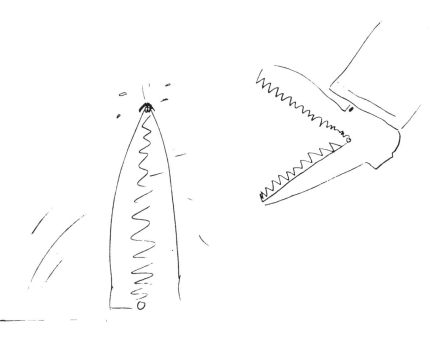

ARMY OFFICER  The point is, when it does break –

SEAGOON  Yes, yes, yes, yes, yes, yes?

ARMY OFFICER  I wish you wouldn't do that! When it breaks, the river Dongler will rise and the fort will be under nine feet of – er – what do you call it –

MATE  Water.

SEAGOON  Gad. What's the answer?

ARMY OFFICER  They'll need underwater gas stoves.

SEAGOON  No such thing's been invented.

ARMY OFFICER  Ah, that's only because nobody has made one. But there is one man.

SEAGOON  One? Come on, there's quite a few of us. Ha! Ha!

ARMY OFFICER  I mean, I know one man who **might** be able to help.

SEAGOON  Not – not – not Dick Scratcher?

ARMY OFFICER  You're dead right – it's not Dick Scratcher. It's Henry Crun – the world's greatest underwater inventor.

ORCHESTRA  *Woeful music*

CRUN  (*sings*) Around the world in eighty-three days, I travelled –

FX  *Knock at door*

MINNIE  I recognise that – it's a knock.

FX  *Knocking*

| | |
|---|---|
| **CRUN** | Come in. |
| **SEAGOON** | Good evening. |
| **MINNIE** | Evening. |
| *FX* | *Door opens and shuts* |
| **CRUN** | I see you beat the door to it. Good evening. |
| **OMNES** | Evening, evening, evening. |
| | (*Pause*) |
| **SEAGOON** | Good evening. |
| **OMNES** | Good evening, evening, evening. |
| **CRUN** | Are you the elephant man? |
| **SEAGOON** | Elephant man? What are you on about? |
| **CRUN** | I'm on about £12 a week. |
| **SEAGOON** | Listen, I'm from the War Office. |
| **CRUN** | War? No thank you, we've just had one! |
| **SEAGOON** | I'm here on a mission. – |
| *FX* | *Tambourine & tuba accompaniment* |
| **CRUN and MINNIE** | (*sing*) Come and join us, come and join us . . . |
| **SEAGOON** | Wrong – wrong – wrong mission! Mr Crun – |
| **CRUN** | Yes. |

| | |
|---|---|
| **SEAGOON** | Can you invent a waterproof military gas stove for cooking ample? |
| **CRUN** | A waterproof gas stove? It's going to be very difficult. You see, you can't get the wood, you know. Can't get it. |
| **SEAGOON** | Have you ever built such a thing before? |
| **CRUN** | Well, in a manner of speaking – **no.** You can't get the wood, you see. |
| **SEAGOON** | Is there no way? |
| **CRUN** | Yes, definitely, definitely, there is! But it will be difficult. |
| **SEAGOON** | Why? |
| **CRUN** | Because you can't get the wood. |
| **SEAGOON** | I can get you the wood. |
| **CRUN** | Ah well, that's going to be very difficult. |
| **SEAGOON** | Why? |
| **CRUN** | I won't be able to go around saying 'You can't get the wood' anymore. |
| *FX* | *Strange unearthly metallic sound* |
| **SEAGOON** | Gracious, what's that? |
| **CRUN** | That's Min playing a gas stove. |
| **SEAGOON** | Ah! How long would it take you to waterproof one? |
| **CRUN** | Well, that depends on how much you'd be willing to pay. |

**SEAGOON**   Thirty thousand pounds!

    **FX**   *Construction noise at colossal high speed, running footsteps, shouts and yells*

**CRUN**   (*exhausted*) Where's the money?

**SEAGOON**   It is **waterproof?**

**CRUN**   We'll soon find out. Min –

**MINNIE**   What is it, ducky?

**CRUN**   Min, just get into the gas oven, would you.

    **FX**   *Door closes*

**MINNIE**   (*echo*) What have you put all these potatoes in with me for, Henry?

**CRUN**   Just in case, Min.

**MINNIE**   (*echo*) In case of what, Henry?

**CRUN**   Yes, in case of what. Mr Seagoon, help me throw this into the river.

    **FX**   *Splash. Bubbles*

**CRUN**   Min!

**MINNIE**   (*echo*) Yes, Henry?

**CRUN**   Are the potatoes still dry?

**MINNIE**   (*echo*) Yes, Henry.

**CRUN**   Hooray, it's working.

MINNIE    That's more than British Leyland.

SEAGOON    Brilliant, Mr Crun. I'll order one right away.

CRUN    How many ones?

SEAGOON    One one.

CRUN    One one? Oh dear, it's a lot of work making one one. Couldn't you order **one** one **one** one **one**?

SEAGOON    Alright – one, one one one one.

CRUN    I just remembered –

SEAGOON    What?

CRUN    You can't get the wood, you see.

SEAGOON    Very well, I'll take the one you just made.

MINNIE    (*off*) Helppp!

CRUN    Too late, it's drifting away down the stream.

| | |
|---|---|
| **SEAGOON** | Quick – follow that gas stove – |
| *FX* | *Splash as body enters water* |
| **MINNIE** | (*distant*) Help! Help! Save me and the potatoes! |
| **SEAGOON** | (*swimming*) Hold on, Madam . . . (*fade*) |
| ***MAX AND ORCHESTRA*** | *Music* |
| **WALLACE** | While Secombe rescued the prototype – Min and the potatoes – Henry Crun struggled manfully with making a second waterproof gas stove. Within a month Captain Seagoon and his gas stoves arrived at the base camp in Africa to arrange transport with a military band. |
| *GRAMS* | *Military brass band music* |
| **BLOODNOK** | Ah Seagoon, bad news – I've got a temperature, but I'm going to carry on. |
| **SEAGOON** | What is your temperature? |
| **BLOODNOK** | 98.4. |
| **SEAGOON** | That's normal. |
| **BLOODNOK** | I know, that's why I'm carrying on. |
| **SEAGOON** | Good. Now, how are we to get the waterproof gas stoves from here to the garrison? Helicopter? |
| **BLOODNOK** | Impossible, sir, impossible. The fort is invisible from the air. And worse still – the air is invisible from the fort. |
| **SEAGOON** | By road, then? |

**BLOODNOK**   No road.

**SEAGOON**   The river?

**BLOODNOK**   No.

**SEAGOON**   Down the river?

**BLOODNOK**   No.

**SEAGOON**   Across the river into the trees?

**BLOODNOK**   No.

**SEAGOON**   Why not?

**BLOODNOK**   No trees.

**SEAGOON**   Across the trees into the river?

**BLOODNOK**   No river.

**SEAGOON**   Rail?

**BLOODNOK**   Doesn't run.

**SEAGOON**   Why not?

**BLOODNOK**   No railway.

**SEAGOON**   Could we build one?

**BLOODNOK**   The river would wash it away.

**SEAGOON**   You said there was no river.

**BLOODNOK**   It's behind the trees.

Goon bird

**SEAGOON**     A moment ago you said there weren't any trees.

**BLOODNOK**     Ah, they've grown since then. Time can't stand still for you, you know.

**SEAGOON**     Wait! I remember seeing an armoured train at the depot.

**BLOODNOK**     That train was only armoured from the inside.

**SEAGOON**     Why?

**BLOODNOK**     We couldn't fire out, but they could fire in.

BBC

**SEAGOON**   Why was that?

**BLOODNOK**   The windows faced inwards.

**SEAGOON**   Then we'll use that!

*FX*   *Guard's train whistle. Engine hooter – train puffs out of station*

**BLOODNOK**   Now, to keep the engine driver alert I've brought me bagpipes –

*FX*   *Bagpipes drone into life*

**SEAGOON**   Why didn't we think of that before? Meanwhile, at Fort Knight –

(*From now on very fast*)

*FX*   *Gunfire, bugles*

**SPIKE**   Meanwhile, Mr Crun –

**CRUN**   You can't get the wood, you know.

**SEAGOON**   Yes! yes! Meanwhile, back in Fort Knight –

*FX*   *Gunfire, bugles*

**SEAGOON**   On the armoured train –

*FX*   *Train and bagpipes*

**BLOODNOK**   We shall have to use electrified Mongolian bagpipes.

**SEAGOON**   Why didn't we think of that before? Meanwhile, at Fort Knight –

| | |
|---|---|
| *FX* | *Gunfire, bugles* |
| **SPIKE** | While back with Crun – |
| **CRUN** | . . . the wood, you know. |
| **SEAGOON** | . . . Fort Knight – |
| *FX* | *Gunfire, bugles* |
| **SPIKE** | At this very moment in London's West End – |
| *GRAMS* | *Victor Sylvester's 'Come Dancing' music* |
| **SEAGOON** | On the armoured train – |
| *FX* | *Train – bagpipes* |
| **SPIKE** | Meantime in Chapter Two! |
| *FX* | *Phone rings* |
| **BLOODNOK** | Hello? Armoured train. |
| *FX* | *Tom-toms* |
| **NATIVE** | (*distorted*) Listen, Bloodnok. This Chief of Biguns Tribe. I give you warning. If you proceed with waterproof gas stove at Fort Knight, we poison the drinking water ... Ha! ha! he! he! |
| **BLOODNOK** | You over-acting swine! |
| **SEAGOON** | Keep him on the line. |
| *FX* | *Whoosh* |

| | |
|---|---|
| **BLOODNOK** | Right. Listen, you devil – |
| **NATIVE** | (*distorted*) I kill everything in your body, I put spear – |
| *FX* | *Pistol shot* |
| **NATIVE** | Argghhh! |
| **SEAGOON** | (*on phone*) Bloodnok? |
| **BLOODNOK** | Yes. |
| **SEAGOON** | I've got him! |

**BLOODNOK**   Splendid. Now get back here right away. Crun's just arrived with an improved waterproof gas stove Mark II.

*ORCHESTRA*   *Dramatic chords*

**WALLACE**   Hurrying overland, Crun reached base camp disguised as a bale of tobacco.

**SEAGOON**   Crun, you've arrived in the nicotine!

*FX*   *Tearing paper wrapper*

**CRUN**   Look – voilà!

SEAGOON   That's not a voilà! That's the stove.

CRUN   Yes. I'll just get in and turn on the gas and set the regulo at 3.

FX   *Switch*

GRAMS   *Organ music: Reginald Dixon's 'I do like to be beside the seaside'*

CRUN   (*echo*) Dear, dear, that's not right. I'll try regulo 2. I'll just have a look inside the oven . . .

FX   *Door opens*

GRAMS   *Railway station noises*

TANNOY   The train now standing at Platform 3 . . .

WELSHMAN   Pardon me, but where's the taxi rank?

CRUN   I'm sorry, I'm a stranger round here.

WELSHMAN   Oh! Where do you come from?

CRUN   Africa.

WELSHMAN   Oh. Would you mind closing the oven door, there's a draught in the waiting-room.

FX   *Door closing*

CRUN   Amazing. Let me see. I think I can see what the trouble is. I had the regulo on 5. It should have been on 2. Now let's see what we get.

QUARTET   *Music*

CRUN    No, there's still something wrong!

SEAGOON    Crun! We can't waste time like this!

CRUN    You know a better way?

SEAGOON    Yes – here it comes. We **must** get to the fort. There's very little time left or right! Bloodnok!

BLOODNOK    He must mean me!

SEAGOON    We must set off immediately.

BLOODNOK    You're dead right. We must do it today, or we'll never get another chance. Eccles, help me get these gas stoves on your head.

ECCLES    Plenty of room. OK. How far do I have to carry them?

BLOODNOK    A thousand miles.

ECCLES    I got to walk all the way?

BLOODNOK    No. Part of the way you'll be allowed to run.

ECCLES    You bastard! (*Censored*)

SEAGOON    Bloodnok, we have to keep this expedition a closely-guarded secret.

BLOODNOK    Don't worry. The camels are all disguised as men.

SEAGOON    And the men?

BLOODNOK    Heavily disguised as camels.

| | |
|---|---|
| **SEAGOON** | Were you trained at MI5? |
| **BLOODNOK** | As a dustman! |
| **SEAGOON** | What a disguise. |
| *ORCHESTRA* | *Safari music – dramatic chords* |
| **SEAGOON** | Thus began a remarkable march of forty-seven days. Forty-seven days **is** remarkable for the month of March. |
| **BLOODNOK** | To conserve energy we marched lying down and only stood up to sleep. |
| **SEAGOON** | Meanwhile, at Fort Knight |
| | *(Silence)* — |
| **ECCLES** | Early closing! |
| *FX* | *African drums* |
| **BLOODNOK** | That night amid the sound of jungle drums, we were confronted by the Biguns natives, some in warpaint, some more civilized in wallpaper. As we neared the Fort we became familiar with African customs. |
| **AFRICAN** | Anything to declare, white man? |
| **BLOODNOK** | A waterproof gas stove. |
| **AFRICAN** | Ymblum naba blum. Importation of gas stove you pay three elephant tusks. |
| **BLOODNOK** | Where do you expect me, from Catford SE6, to get elephant tusks? |

■ ■ ■ ■ ■ ■ ■ ■ ■ ■ ■ ■ ■ ■

**AFRICAN**    I sell you.

**BLOODNOK**    How much?

**AFRICAN**    One waterproof gas stove.

**BLOODNOK**    What luck! Eccles, give him one of the waterproof gas stoves.

**AFRICAN**    Here – tusks.

    **FX**    *Crashing of tusks*

Jack Oakley

| | |
|---|---|
| ECCLES | Oh. Now he's got a waterproof gas stove. |
| BLOODNOK | What luck. **Just** what we need. I say, tribal fellow, how much you want for waterproof gas stove? |
| AFRICAN | Three elephant tusks. |
| BLOODNOK | Three? Just what we've got – |
| SEAGOON | News from Fort Knight! They've only enough uncooked ample for another hour. |
| BLOODNOK | Well, it's only eighteen miles as the crow flies, but our crow is sick with lurgi. |
| SEAGOON | Eighteen miles, through native tribes. It means certain death or certain life. |
| BLOODNOK | Yes. One of us must volunteer. |
| SEAGOON | Yes, one of us must volunteer. |
| ECCLES | One of us **must** volunteer. |
| BLOODNOK | Good old Eccles. |
| ECCLES | No. Bad old Eccles. |
| SEAGOON | Brave boy, Eccles. |
| ECCLES | No, coward Eccles. |
| SEAGOON | You coward. |
| ECCLES | I'm a coward. |

| | |
|---|---|
| **BLOODNOK** | You coward. |
| **ECCLES** | You coward. |
| **SEAGOON** | You coward. |
| **BLOODNOK** | Well it's no good **three** cowards going. |
| **SEAGOON** | (*calls*) Mr Crun! Mr Crun, we have one hour in which to cover eighteen miles to the fort. Any suggestions? |
| **CRUN** | Well, we could go by train. That's regulo 5. |
| *FX* | *Switch* |
| **SEAGOON** | Good. Open the oven door! |
| *FX* | *Door opens. Sound of trains* |
| **TANNOY** | Train now standing at Platform 7 of the gas stove, is for Fort Knight. |
| **CRUN** | (*echo*) Just in time. Everybody into the gas stove. I'll get in first. Come on. Hand me in the right side of the stove. Now the left. Now the top and the back. Now close the oven door from the outside and bring it in after you. |
| **ECCLES** | Wait a minute. Close it on the outside? And bring it in after me? That would mean climbing through it when it's shut and not opening it till I get through. |
| **SEAGOON** | Well? What are you waiting for? |
| **ECCLES** | I don't know how to do it. |

| | |
|---|---|
| **SEAGOON** | We'll take the rest of the oven by train. **You** get the oven door and go ahead on foot. Is that all clear? |
| **ECCLES** | Er – |
| **SEAGOON** | Good. Swallow this road map and follow the instructions. |
| *ORCHESTRA* | *Dramatic chords* |
| **SEAGOON** | Within an hour we were at the gates of Fort Knight. |
| *FX* | *Gunfire, bugles. Native warriors* |
| **CRUN** | I'll ring. |
| *FX* | *Doorbell* |
| **SEAGOON** | I'll do the talking. I've got an 11-plus, you just look intelligent. |
| **ECCLES** | Oh dear. |
| *FX* | *Door opens* |
| **BUTLER** | Was that **you** ringing, sir? |
| **SEAGOON** | No, it was the bell. We'd like to speak to the commanding officer. |
| **BUTLER** | I'll see if he's in, sir. |
| *FX* | *Door closes* |
| **SEAGOON** | He was a nice fellow – I wonder why he was nude. |
| *FX* | *Door opens* |

**BUTLER** Pardon me, sir, they're rather busy at the moment. If you could leave your card?

**SEAGOON** My card? It's in my other suit.

**BUTLER** Perhaps you'd like to stay to tea, sir.

**SEAGOON** Oh, that is kind.

**BUTLER** You must excuse the confusion, we have the enemies of the Queen here.

**SEAGOON** Oh, are they stopping here as well?

**BUTLER** Yes. It's all very confusing at mealtimes. Is yours the waterproof gas stove we're expecting?

**SEAGOON** Yes. Could we connect it to the mains?

**BUTLER** I'm afraid that would serve no purpose.

**SEAGOON** What do you mean?

**BUTLER** The gas was cut off yesterday. A matter of a quarter in arrears.

**SEAGOON** Never mind. We mustn't fail now. Eccles, open that brown paper parcel.

**ECCLES** (*sings as opens parcel*) Oh! It's you!

**BLUEBOTTLE** Yes, I've seen the light, Captain. I'm the rescue plan. Hello, everybody. I heard you call.

**SEAGOON** I haven't called yet.

| BLUEBOTTLE | I'm answering in advance. Strikes answering-in-advance pose, well forward on balls of feet. |
|---|---|
| SEAGOON | Get into the gas stove and connect this cylinder of gas. |
| BLUEBOTTLE | Yes, I will, Captain. I will do that. Enters gas stove, and assumes crouching position within, as assumed by certain people in *Bridge over the River Kwai,* playing South London all next week. Fixes gas cylinder. Here, I smell gas. |
| SEAGOON | Can you see where the leak is? |
| BLUEBOTTLE | No, it's very dark in here. |
| SEAGOON | Well, strike a match. |
| BLUEBOTTLE | All right, Captain. Oh, wait a minute. Are you sure this match will not ignite the gas, thereby deading me, as it has on many previous occasions? |
| WALLACE | Listeners, stand by for the obvious. |
| SEAGOON | Of course not. They're safety matches. |
| BLUEBOTTLE | Thank you for your words of comfort, Captain. I trust you with my life. I do do that, yes. I will strike a match now. Strikes safety match for safety. |
| FX | *Strikes match* |
| BLUEBOTTLE | Ah-hah! You're waiting for me to get deaded, aren't you? But I'm not going to. This week Bluebottle is not going to be deaded. So there. |

| | |
|---|---|
| **FX** | *Explosion, followed by knock on door. Door opens* |
| **POSTMAN** | Brown paper parcel for you, sir. |
| **ECCLES** | Thank you. |
| **FX** | *Paper being torn off parcel* |
| **ECCLES** | Oh – it's you! |
| **BLUEBOTTLE** | You rotten swine, you! Seeks among debris for shattered underpants, shredded boots and three 1″ by 1½″ lumps of head. |
| **SEAGOON** | But, lad – you've done it! |
| **BUTLER** | Compliments of the besieged garrison, sir, could you make your explosions quieter? We can't hear ourselves fight. |
| **SEAGOON** | Don't you realise, below stairs fool, the underwater gas stove has exploded! |
| **BUTLER** | Oh dear, and I had the Sunday joint all ready. This will mean surrender to the enemies of the Queen. |
| **SEAGOON** | Surrender? |
| **BUTLER** | Surrender. |
| **BLOODNOK** | Surrender? |
| **SEAGOON** | To the enemies of the Queen? |
| **BLOODNOK** | A splendid idea, I'll put my coward set on! |

**SEAGOON**  No! Go in there and fight. Give out the swords. Open that gate and we'll charge.

**FX**  *Door opens*

**SEAGOON**  Charge! Wait! There's nobody here.

**BLOODNOK**  They've all gone.

**ECCLES**  There's not a soul.

**SEAGOON**  What a disappointing ending to a show.

**WALLACE**  Perhaps listeners will now believe how bad things really are in the Old Country. Good night.

BBC

# The Raspberry Song

The Goons' very last recording, 1979. The
'Raspberry Song' for Decca Records

```
In a little town where I belong,
There's a most accomplished fellow.
He's the leader of the village choir,
And his voice is warm and mellow.
He drives a fruit cart round the street
And everybody knows it:
He doesn't sing or rave about
His fruit, he simply blows it

XXX XXX XXX XXX XXX - 'raspberry'

He's doing it all day long

XXX XXX XXX XXX XXX
```

*Peter Sellers demonstrating how to hold up a bank,
while Milligan holds up a sandwich*

# The Raspberry Song

In a little town where I belong, There's a most accomplished fellow.

He's the leader of the village choir, And his voice is warm and mellow. He

drives a fruit cart round the street And everybody knows it: He

doesn't sing or rave about His fruit, he simply blows it

(Orchestra) (Raspberry...) He's doing it all day long

(Raspberry...) It's better than any song, Though it isn't very pretty You've

got to admit it's cute So, all together, let it go (Raspberry...) Eat more fruit

(Raspberry...) It's certainly come to stay (Raspberry...)

It's a treat to hear him say, Hey Fruit's in season, plenty there is:

Apples, plums & the old raspberries (Raspberry...) Everything is fresh today

It's better than any song,
Though it isn't very pretty
You've got to admit it's cute
So, all together, let it go

XXX XXX XXX XXX XXX

Eat more fruit

XXX XXX XXX XXX XXX

It's certainly come to stay

XXX XXX XXX XXX XXX

It's a treat to hear him say, Hey
Fruit's in season, plenty there is:
Apples, plums and the old raspberries

*Sir Harry Secombe reading the word 'laugh' from a piece of paper*

XXX XXX XXX XXX XXX

Everything is fresh today.


Every Friday night when work is done,
He never wastes a minute.
To the village hall he hurries round
Where he sings just like a linnet.
To hear him blow a melody
It's great, you can't deny it;
And if you've nothing else to do
I'd like you all to try it.

XXX XXX XXX XXX XXX

Get ready and do it now.

XXX XXX XXX XXX XXX

It's easy when you know how.
Though it isn't very pretty
You've got to admit it's cute
So, all together, let it go

XXX XXX XXX XXX XXX

Eat more fruit

XXX XXX XXX XXX XXX

It's certainly come to stay

XXX XXX XXX XXX XXX

It's a treat to hear him say, Hey
So Te La So Fa Me Re Doh

It's a treat to hear him say
Fruit's in season, plenty there is:
Apples, plums and the old raspberries

XXX XXX XXX XXX XXX

XXX XXX XXX XXX XXX

Everything is fresh today

Everything is fresh today.

It's certainly come to stay

XXX XXX XXX XXX XXX

*Spike Milligan telling Sir Harry Secombe how big his is*

Jack Oakley

▲ ▲ ▲ ▲ ▲ ▲ ▲ ▲ ▲ ▲ ▲ ▲ ▲

# THE TREE MANIAC

The Tree Maniac.

Announcer: Good evening, the BBC Home Service presents the Grünes ( pause) Grunes? Grunes??? Yes, it's quite definitely written here: G-R-U-N-E-S. Of course, they must mean Coons - yes, that's it - Coons (walks away repeating)

John Snagge (Peter) Mr Greenslade is currently being treated by Sir Charles Fees the famous Psychiatrist and used car salesman. What Greenslade meant to say was that Thisis the Grute Show (Pause) Grute?, no h + G they mean _ Grune - the Grune Show
[Long Silence]

Oboe    Gives hurried tuning A to Orchestra

Snagge   Bai Jove I do believe they werent quite ready - Have another try Ladies and .

Orchestra   Come in too soon with signature tune.
[Pause]

FX      Fork falls on floor

This really was a Lost Goon Show – lost, forgotten and never finished. This is its very first public appearance.

ANNOUNCER    Good evening, the BBC Home Service presents the Grunes (*Pause*) Grunes? **Grunes**??? Yes, it's quite definitely written here: G-R-U-N-E-S. Of course, they must mean Coons – yes, that's it – Coons (*walks away repeating*)

JOHN SNAGGE    (**Peter**) Mr Greenslade is currently being treated by Sir Charles Fees, the famous psychiatrist and used car salesman. What Greenslade meant to say was that this is the **Grute** Show. (*Pause*) Grute? No, ladies and gentlemen, they mean Grune – the Grune Show. (*Long silence*)

OBOE    *Gives hurried tuning A to Orchestra*

SNAGGE    Bai Jove, I do believe they weren't quite ready. Have another try: ladies and –

ORCHESTRA    *Come in too soon with signature tune*

(*Pause*)

FX    *Fork falls on floor*

NED SEAGOON    That thrilling sound of an EPNS fork hitting the ground signals the start of a mysterious mystery.

▲ ▲ ▲ ▲ ▲ ▲ ▲ ▲ ▲ ▲ ▲ ▲ ▲ ▲

| | |
|---|---|
| **SPIKE** | *(starter)* On your marks – get set – |
| *FX* | *Starter's pistol, followed by mass of boots running away* |
| **NED** | Very well, I do it on my own – ladies and gentlemen, The Landing Tree Maniac. |
| **ORCHESTRA** | *Brooding-mystery chords mixed with maniacal laughter and tree chopping* |
| **DIMBLEBY** | **(Peter)** The Queen places the Royal sapling in the Royal hole and with a silver shovel fills it in. |
| **THE QUEEN** | **(Peter)** I name this tree Copper Beech. God bless its nuts, and all who will assail her. |
| *FX* | *Feeble clapping* |
| **ANNOUNCER** | Meantime – at Catford police station a Constable Oaf is at work beating a rubber bust of Cliff Richard. |
| *FX* | *Truncheon on head* |
| **CONSTABLE** | **(Spike** – Cockney) Take that, you hippy swine. |
| *FX* | *Truncheon wallop* |
| **CONSTABLE** | Earnin' orl that money. |
| *FX* | *Wallop* |
| **CONSTABLE** | Singing crappy tunes! |
| *FX* | *Wallop* |
| **CONSTABLE** | And me with my fine voice on only 18 quid a week. |
| *FX* | *Wallop. Phone rings* |

▲ ▲ ▲ ▲ ▲ ▲ ▲ ▲ ▲ ▲ ▲ ▲ ▲

**CONSTABLE**   Hello – Hello – better pick it up, but first –

        *FX*   *Wallop. Picks phone up*

**CONSTABLE**   Catford Police Station.

    **NEDDY**   Hello, this is Neddy Seagoon, Welsh midget and Forester-in-waiting to the Queen!

**CONSTABLE**   Oh, you ever seen that swine Cliff Richard – he gets £2,000,000 a minute.

        *FX*   *Wallop*

    **NEDDY**   Yes – I want to report –

**ANNOUNCER**   The BBC would like to point that what you are hearing is not typical of the police force. The Inspector has said he personally is not jealous of Cliff Richard – it's that bastard Elvis Presley –

**NEDDY**   It's true – the £18-a-week police were not interested, folks – so I would have to go to the £10 a week police, even 9 or 8! Nine and eight make £17, that would be only a pound cheaper than the £18 a week, understand? (*Gibbers on*)

**ANNOUNCER**   Mr Seagoon is also being treated by Sir Charles Fees.

**NEDDY**   So money is no object – I'll just throw this shilling on the pavement to see if there's any Scotsmen in the district.

**FX**   *Shilling on pavement followed by approach of two sets of boot at speed. They halt*

**GRYTPYPE-THYNNE**   (*breathless*) M'card!

**NEDDY**   MacHard – ah – a real Scot! See, Thynne & Moriarty, financiers and 24-hour dry cleaners.

**CONSTABLE**   And me only £18 a week –

**FX**   *Wallop*

**NEDDY**   Listen, constabule of old Catford, I wish to report a tree vandal –

**CONSTABLE**   Oh – is it a doggie?

**NEDDY**   Is what a doggie?

| | |
|---|---|
| **CONSTABLE** | (*barks*) Bow-wow-wow-woof-grrr- |
| **NEDDY** | What's that? |
| **CONSTABLE** | That's a doggie! |
| **NEDDY** | I thought you were a policeman. |
| **CONSTABLE** | I am, and it's only £18 a week. |
| *FX* | *Wallop* |
| **NEDDY** | Look, you know Herne's Mighty Oak in Windsor Park? |
| **CONSTABLE** | Well, not personally. |
| **NEDDY** | Well, it's – |
| **CONSTABLE** | – and he's always havin' it off with good-lookin' birds – |
| *FX* | *Wallop* |
| **NEDDY** | Look, man! Herne's Mighty Oak has been uprooted – roots and all! |
| **CONSTABLE** | – and 'e's not even good lookin'! |
| *FX* | *Wallop (continues)* |
| **MORIARTY** | Owww! |
| **NEDDY** | The sound came from a shivering wreck wearing a wedding-tackle-length vest, a topless bowler – and a reconditioned cricketer's box – lying stretched on the pavement. |

▲ ▲ ▲ ▲ ▲ ▲ ▲ ▲ ▲ ▲ ▲ ▲ ▲ ▲ ▲

**THYNNE**  My partner, Count Jim 'Knackered' Moriarty – a scion of Grade 3 Salmon, has played the lead in several French post-cards.

**NEDDY**  Is he dead?

**THYNNE**  That is a trade secret – but his strength is unbounded – with him we can crack this case open.

**NEDDY**  So saying he cracked a case open –

**FX**  *Case being smashed*

**THYNNE**  That's just a beginning – you want Herne's Mighty Oak traced?

**NEDDY**  Yes yes yes yes yes yes!

**THYNNE**  One yes would have done – you're used to working with the deaf or the Irish? Moriarty, cover me with a song.

**MORIARTY**  (*sings*) These teeth are the teeth of a woman in love. (*Continues*)

**THYNNE**  Neddy – so far, our investigations have led us to this blank cheque – it would help our enquiries if you signed just here.

**FX**  *Hurried signing*

**THYNNE**  What a beautiful hand –

**MORIARTY**  Yes – but a terrible signature.

**THYNNE**  Moriarty, open the Cyprus Sherry.

▲▲▲▲▲▲▲▲▲▲▲▲▲▲

| | |
|---|---|
| *FX* | *Pop and pouring* |
| NEDDY | It – it looks like water! |
| THYNNE | A toast to your forthcoming overdraft. |
| *FX* | *Clinking glasses* |
| NEDDY | It – it **tastes** like water! |
| THYNNE | Water? There's an old Latin adage: Parventum – ad hoc – nil desperandum – aqua frescha! |
| NEDDY | Oh – I wish I'd met you earlier. |
| THYNNE | So do we, Neddy – say so do we for me, Moriarty. |
| MORIARTY | So do we! |
| *FX* | *Terrible slap* |
| MORIARTY | Ow – mon tête! |
| NEDDY | Why do you keep hitting him? |
| THYNNE | Why? Because he's **there**! |
| ANNOUNCER | Who would want to remove Herne's Oak? The first clue came from a couple living in Neasden. |
| *FX* | *Clock ticking – bed springs – snoring. Alarm clock rings.* |
| CRUN & BANNISTER | *(waking noises)* |
| CRUN | I'll just look in the mirror . . . Oh. Is it open eyes for awake? |
| BANNISTER | Well, that's how I do it! |

▲ ▲ ▲ ▲ ▲ ▲ ▲ ▲ ▲ ▲ ▲ ▲ ▲ 157

**CRUN**    Ah!

**BANNISTER**    Ooooo! Are you awake, Henry?

**CRUN**    What's the time?

**BANNISTER**    I set the alarm for three.

**CRUN**    Why? There's only two of us.

**BANNISTER**    There must be six more somewhere –

**FX**    *Bong of po*

**CRUN**    Oh –

**BANNISTER**    It's very dark this morning. Look how dark it is out.

**CRUN**    That's the blinds, Min.

**FX**    *Sound of doorknob, and bolts being withdrawn*

**CRUN**    (*off mike*) Oh, Min. There's something on the landing.

**BANNISTER**    It must be the cat.

**CRUN**    No, a cat couldn't do this. Someone's left an oak tree on the landing. Cats can't do oak trees.

**BANNISTER**    Let me see. Oh, there's a label on it – 'From the Tree Maniac'.

**CRUN**    I don't remember ordering a tree from a maniac.

**BANNISTER**    It must be a joke.

**CRUN**    No, Min, it's not a joke. It's definitely a tree. Jokes don't have leaves on.

▲ ▲ ▲ ▲ ▲ ▲ ▲ ▲ ▲ ▲ ▲ ▲ ▲ ▲

| | |
|---|---|
| **BANNISTER** | No, some jokes have whiskers on. |
| **BOTH** | _Talk at cross purposes – fade_ |
| **FX** | _Heavy snoring_ |
| **ANNOUNCER** | The snoring you hear is that of the duty fireman at Lewisham. |
| **FX** | _Phone rings – snorer wakes up_ |
| **FIREMAN** | (**Spike**) Hello, Lewisham fire brigade. |
| **CRUN** | Hello – we have a tree on our landing. |
| **FIREMAN** | Thanks for telling me. |
| **CRUN** | Don't go – we want help. |
| **FIREMAN** | Well, is the tree on fire? |
| **CRUN** | No. |
| **FIREMAN** | Well, we can't come unless it's on fire. |
| **CRUN** | Min, he says he can't come unless the tree is on fire. |
| **BANNISTER** | Oh. I'll get a box of matches. |
| **CRUN** | If you come now, we'll have it going by the time you arrive. |
| **FIREMAN** | It's very nice of you to put work my way. |

**(and here it ends)**

▲ ▲ ▲ ▲ ▲ ▲ ▲ ▲ ▲ ▲ ▲ ▲ ▲ ▲